Praise for *The Insight Cure*

"Dr. Sharp is a brilliant and articulate physician. He is an extraordinarily gifted teacher and passionate about helping people. *The Insight Cure* is filled with much wisdom and compelling stories."

— **Sanjiv Chopra, M.D.**, professor of medicine at
Harvard Medical School, best-selling author,
and inspirational speaker

"Mental health is an issue close to my heart. There is a staggering need for more information, education, and application of better mental health in America. We need more outstanding physicians who are smart and passionate, clever and caring. Dr. John Sharp is one of those physicians. He tunes in to a patient's unique individuality and guides the way to healing. Dr. Sharp stands out in his field as truly a 'doctor's doctor.'"

— **Kristen Bell**, actor, *The Good Place, Veronica Mars, Frozen,*
and *House of Lies*

"In the 30 years I have known Dr. John Sharp, I have rarely encountered a colleague with his combination of insight, warmth, and creativity. Beyond his excellence in caring for the person, he brings to his work an astounding breadth of knowledge and wisdom, and his writing is practical and engaging."

— **John M. Talmadge, M.D.**, senior medical advisor, Brain
Performance Institute at the Center for BrainHealth;
clinical professor of psychiatry & addiction medicine
at the University of Texas at Dallas

THE

INSIGHT
CURE

ALSO BY JOHN SHARP

The Emotional Calendar

THE
INSIGHT
CURE

CHANGE YOUR STORY,
TRANSFORM YOUR LIFE

———

JOHN SHARP, M.D.

HAY HOUSE, INC.
Carlsbad, California • New York City
London • Sydney • Johannesburg
Vancouver • New Delhi

Published and distributed in the United States by: Hay House, Inc.: www
.hayhouse.com® • **Published and distributed in Australia by:** Hay House
Australia Pty. Ltd.: www.hayhouse.com.au • **Published and distributed in the
United Kingdom by:** Hay House UK, Ltd.: www.hayhouse.co.uk • **Distributed in
Canada by:** Raincoast Books: www.raincoast.com • **Published in India by:** Hay
House Publishers India: www.hayhouse.co.in

Cover design: Ploy Siripant • *Interior design:* Riann Bender
Indexer: Joan D. Shapiro • *Interior illustrations:* Grace Tobin

Cataloging-in-Publication Data is on file at the Library of Congress

Hardcover ISBN: 978-1-4019-5324-9

10 9 8 7 6 5 4 3 2 1
1st edition, February 2018

Printed in the United States of America

To my mom and my dad

————————

CONTENTS

INTRODUCTION

The word *truth* is overused in our culture these days. People claim to be "truth tellers" or to "speak their truth." But for most of us, our truth—our sense of self, our assessment of our abilities, our assumptions about the way things play out, and our concept of how we fit into the world—is founded on a lie.

If you've ever said, "I don't know why I do it, but I can't help myself," your truth is false.

If you make the same mistakes over and over again or have noticed that certain situations trigger intense reactions that overwhelm or paralyze you, your truth is false.

If you are stuck in a rut—in your career, marriage, weight, or habits—your truth is false.

You have been telling yourself one central "false truth" since you were a very young child. It was installed in your mind at a time of life when you didn't know the difference between a healthy and an unhealthy reaction to something that scared or upset you. You just felt bad, and you self-soothed by telling yourself a story. The story was about you and how you should change your actions or assumptions about yourself and other people in order to feel safe. Since the story gave you comfort at the time, you told it to yourself over and over again, so many times that it played like a loop in your head. By now, you've stopped even hearing it, but it's still in there, still playing, decades later. In psychological terms, this story is your *unconscious narrative*. And it's a lie.

This unconscious narrative has shaped your psychology and inhibited you from pursuing life with confidence and strength. You are not all you can be because of it. You can't even imagine all you could be because of it.

Basically, something bad happened—or something you perceived as bad—when you were very young, and it really messed you up. Most people know that childhood sets the stage for adulthood's problems. What most people don't know, however, is what set off the chain of reactions that created the faulty and damaging unconscious narrative. They certainly don't know how to figure it out or how to change their old narrative for a new, better one in order to live a happier, healthier life.

In my 20-plus years of clinical practice, treating hundreds of patients, not one of them could at first accurately identify the false truth that was the root cause of all their suffering.

If you were one of my patients, and I asked you, "What misconception from childhood is still defining you now, as an adult?" would you able to come up with an answer? It's a tough question, absolutely. People look at big-picture problems, like their parents' divorce, a death, or bullying. As important as those things are, they are events that occurred. They're not the big lie you told yourself about your role in the event. The event itself is different from how you changed because of it having happened. Your perception of the event and how it changed your behavior and sense of self are the issues at hand that are still causing problems for you now as an adult.

So what is this big lie?

Figuring out your false truth is the most important work you can do to unlock change in your life. It's been the work of my career to help patients discover the lie that defines them.

One patient referred to me as the "False-Truth Detector." I'll take it.

Why is this work so important? If you discover your false truth, you gain valuable insight. And what, exactly, is insight in a psychological sense?

At its most simple, **insight is the ability to recognize cause and effect**. You already have the superficial insight to recognize that, for example, if you lie to your spouse, you will get in serious trouble when they find out. The lie (cause) leads to trouble (effect). The kind of insight I'm talking about in this book goes much deeper than that. In this example, the cause is actually the false truth formed in childhood that tells you to lie. The lie itself is the effect, and by extension, so are your unstable relationships. By gaining insight, you will have a clear understanding of where your impulse to lie comes from, and from that knowledge, you can work to uproot the cause *and* the effect, the childhood false truth *and* the adult self-sabotaging. When you are insightful about why you do what you do, you can change your behavior to live a healthier, happier life.

Insight can also be an epiphany, a realization when suddenly everything makes sense. For an insight to have a real impact, it has to go back to the false truth from childhood. Once you discover what that is and think about how it has affected your attitude and behavior, you will get that aha! feeling, when the fog lifts and you suddenly see and understand so many things that you couldn't explain before.

Insight is also a superpower that goes by another name: self-awareness. It's really knowing who you are and shedding delusions, filters, and masks. When you have such awareness, you don't hide behind excuses and rationalizations that keep you stuck in ruts. Sometimes the ruts themselves are invisible. Insight reveals those to you too.

With insight, you can begin the process of fundamentally changing your sense of self and become the hero of your own life. You can throw out the old narrative that has been dragging you down, write a new one, live by it, and watch your life transform. No more self-sabotage. No more beating yourself up or shrinking from challenges. No more living with fear, depression, or addiction.

When you are living in the glow of insight, your brain's architecture will change accordingly. Old synapses, wiring-like pathways that were formed and reinforced by repeated bad behavior, will wither. New synapses, forged by healthy habits and thoughts, will grow brighter and deeper, making you a stronger, happier person psychologically and neurologically. Negative self-talk will stop. Positive assumptions and attitudes that lead to wise choices will take its place. Your brain will be reshaped for success.

Insight unlocks potential and jolts you out of stagnation. And it's available and accessible to everyone, no therapist required.

Insight Itself

When I was in residency training at the University of California, San Francisco, I gained valuable insight into insight itself. I was among a small group of advanced residents in psychiatry. In our last semester, nearly four years of postgraduate medical education in, we were evaluated by the head of the outpatient department, who was in many ways the guru of the whole program. Dr. Amini was a classically trained psychoanalyst with a practicality that was unusual at the time. He didn't say very much, but all his words were provocative and on point. He was above all else wise and practical and definitely very deep. A resident was permitted to graduate the training program only when Dr. Amini was satisfied that he or she was indeed competent.

After hitting the books and studying every psychiatric theory from Freud through Gestalt and beyond and reviewing our newly obtained clinical experience, on the day of the evaluation, I was ready for anything.

Dr. Amini came into the room, smiled at the group, and asked his first question: "Who can explain what insight feels like?"

The other residents and I, bewildered, looked at each other and then down at our laps. No one had an answer. I knew what insight *was*—recognition of cause and effect, when everything suddenly makes sense, and deeply felt self-awareness. Sometimes it's described as a flash or a bolt out of the blue. But as a *feeling*, as a physical sensation in the body? I wasn't sure. I hoped the professor wouldn't call on me.

When he saw that all of us were avoiding eye contact with him, he waited. Then eventually he put us out of our misery. "Insight is a sinking feeling," he said.

And then I got that sinking feeling myself. Yes, that was *exactly* what insight felt like. It's not a moment to bounce out of your chair with excitement or to crumble across your desk in despair. Insight is gravity, a profound heaviness in your gut.

In fact, insight is the deepest feeling you can have because it's the foundation of all your experiences. Insight clues you in to *why* you feel sad, angry, frustrated, grateful, or happy in a given situation. Deep understanding allows you to challenge your thoughts and change your behavior.

Until the day I graduated, Dr. Amini was still teaching us about insight and its profound importance.

Also as part of my psychiatric training at UCSF, I felt I had to go into therapy myself. I'd learned a lot of theory in school and I had some clinical experience. But until I started those therapy sessions, I hadn't had much exposure to counseling from the other side of the desk in order to be able to apply the concepts to myself. I was uncomfortable at first, incredibly anxious because I felt so daunted and alone inside. I didn't know what the nature and scope of my underlying issues might truly be. "I know I need to be here," I told my therapist on the first day, but I couldn't tell him why. I remember his warmth and curiosity and confidence as we began the process of discovery.

Like many of my own patients, I had no idea what I didn't know about myself. After several sessions, though, I would figure out my false truth—and how lucky I had been not to let it define me as I grew up to be an adult.

When I was very young, my parents divorced. It was acrimonious. My mother and father were not capable of communicating with each other at all. I went to live with my mom and her parents. If I asked to see or talk to my father, Mom became visibly agitated and usually developed a rash. It seemed to hurt her if I brought him up at all. She was dramatic, and he was reticent. When my father and I did get together, he didn't seem talkative and I couldn't get comfortable with him for fear of upsetting Mom. It's possible he had other interests, or he wasn't very good at relating to a little kid. It's hard to say. (My father and I have sorted things out and have a fine relationship now.) Even though I didn't much enjoy visits with Dad, I wanted more of them. I learned not to ask for them, though, because Mom's distress was overwhelming for me.

My grandparents were wonderful people. My grandfather was a physician and an exquisitely positive role model, but in the family lore, he was a saint and could do no wrong. My mother and grandmother put him on a pedestal. I found him approachable, but he didn't struggle with the worries and anxiety I felt, and I couldn't relate to him as much as I could admire him.

At school, I was shy and insecure and I developed a stutter. My predominant emotions were vulnerability and fear, especially when I compared my feelings with the apparent confidence of others. I was surrounded by love at home from Mom and my grandparents, but I didn't have a relatable male role model and I felt this absence acutely. I was confused about how to act and worried about doing or saying the wrong thing.

My false truth was the belief that I was terrifyingly alone despite being around other people and that I wouldn't prove capable of finding my way through life. Due to my experience of my mom's distress and my father's distance, I grew up stumbling over my words for fear of displeasing the people I counted on for survival. I retreated deeply into myself and at times could barely speak. The stutter was a manifestation of feeling insecure and isolated.

Then, thanks to good luck and my mom's good sense, I was saved from growing up believing the "on my own" false truth. Mom sent me to an all-boys' middle and high school where I found approachable role models in my friends' fathers, my teachers, and my coaches. I saw how these men conducted themselves, and I was able to cobble together an idea of the kind of man I was supposed to be. The lucky part was that the father figures I adopted were all excellent people who generously took me on. In a systematic but unconscious way, I proved to myself that I wasn't "on my own" after all.

In therapy during my training, I got the sinking insightful feeling of understanding the constant ache of my childhood. I realized that if it hadn't been for my motivation and good fortune to find role models, I might still be the middle-aged version of the shy boy with a stutter, afraid to express his needs and wants. My unconscious led me to find role models who made me feel less alone and afraid. I fixed a problem I didn't know I had. Interestingly, I'd done the same thing again in my current situation. When I was initially looking for a therapist to work with, I asked Dr. Amini for suggestions. I asked him to recommend a person who was not only a good psychiatrist but who himself was leading an admirable life. I didn't want a coach who couldn't play the game. Dr. Amini told me that in all his years of "matchmaking" therapists for psychiatry residents in training, he had never been asked that, and he advised me to consider what about that request was particularly important to me and why. I wasn't able to answer his question until much later, but now it is clear that having role models is a particularly important compass point as I navigate life. I needed role models who cared about me in order to get in touch with my own sense of inner adequacy. So there I was, unknowingly seeking out what I knew I needed, yet without any real insight into how that worked.

A cascade of revelations followed therapy, shedding light on my relationships with my parents and on how things might have played out for me if I hadn't gotten lucky. This was huge! The process of insight leading to such discoveries was elegant and profound. I had to learn more about the concept. As I intensely studied theories about insight, I learned that most people aren't as lucky as I was. Most people don't unconsciously correct their childhood false truths. They get stuck with feeling alone, misunderstood, unloved, unworthy, and worthless. Their entire lives are shaped by these common false truths. As a therapist, I set out to relieve patients of their misconceptions and help them move forward unburdened.

Insight can allow you to hit the reset button on life, no matter your age or how entrenched you might be in your old ways. There is no reason you can't get rid of childhood misconceptions and use your adult intelligence to redefine yourself.

The Insight Cure: Eight Steps to Change

Becoming insightful is a process. One step builds on the next. All the steps are absolutely necessary and distinct. To hit the reset button on your life, you have to follow each step *in order* and give it the time and attention it requires. Glossing over a step, skipping ahead, or starting at the end won't get you the optimal relief and results you want.

The progression below is something I developed over decades in clinical practice with my patients. If you made an appointment with me and came to my office, I would work through the process in the same way, in the same order, using the same strategies with the same guidance and support offered on these pages.

Part I of the Insight Cure contains the first three steps and focuses on awareness. Why is change so hard? What might be your childhood misconception? What actual event caused it? How did it develop into an unconscious narrative (a story about who you are, how you fit in, and what you can expect) that has controlled you ever since?

Step one: Understanding why change is hard. Insight begins with the desire to change. You know that you're not happy, and you suspect that life doesn't have to be as much of a struggle as it has been. The desire to change might be strong, but for many reasons, you can't seem to put those wheels into motion. Each of us has substantial psychological obstacles already in place in our brains that prevent us from surging ahead. As much as we want to change, humans are preprogrammed to resist doing so. This first important step is about understanding and acknowledging the forces that keep you locked and blocked. You have to see the obstacle before you can get around it. As an adult who is motivated to change, you can use focused determination to get to the root of your old story.

Step two: Recognizing your false truth. You suffered an early disappointment, loss, or feeling of guilt or shame, and your interpretation of what happened was probably inaccurate because you were a child. You internalized the misconception and adjusted your behavior in accordance to it—out of necessity, you believed.

The false truth turned into a story, the central, unconscious narrative in your life, a pattern of anticipatory ideas and expectations that has become a self-fulfilling prophecy. The goal of this step is to formulate a general idea about your unconscious narrative by examining your life philosophy, set of assumptions, and how you use language to talk yourself out of the behavior you don't want and into the behavior you do want.

Step three: Tracing the false truth's origins. Although it's not absolutely necessary to pinpoint the exact moment your false truth began—it's impossible for most of us to remember that far back—it is possible to approximate the timing and using a series of exercises, to form an accurate picture about how and when it got started.

Part II of the Insight Cure is made up of three steps devoted to dismantling your unconscious narrative—that old story about who you are, how you fit in, and how the world works—and building a new story for yourself.

Step four: Reflecting on the old story. Your unconscious narrative was constructed on a shaky foundation, to say the least. As a child, you didn't know anything about nuances in relationships or life. You were defenseless, and your shield against pain was a protective false truth. Now that you're an adult, you can see subtle shades of meaning. You're no longer defenseless, and you don't need to hold on to that shield anymore. During this step, you'll revisit specific experiences and events from the near and distant past to see, in the blazing light of insight, how the false truth controlled your actions and reactions. It can be painful to relive important events, but in order to destroy the old story, you have to fully appreciate how the consequences of your false truth have played out in your life.

Step five: Working through the old story. This step will help you gain a mentality of reality for an even deeper understanding of what's really happening and of the choices you make. You will take a giant leap forward by learning to look at the past as an observer of it, seeing yourself objectively. To learn from the past, you have to remove the emotions from it and see things as they really are from multiple perspectives. You'll learn the important skills of forgiving yourself and others and separating decisively from the old narrative.

Step six: Building your new story. To make the journey from the familiar world of your false truth to the extraordinary new world, you need a new sense of self. Your "new narrative" is the story of objective reality. Who are you, really? What are your virtues, strengths, skills? You get to construct your new narrative from the ground up, based on what you're genuinely good at. Constructing a new story is not about making a vision board with pictures of a mansion and a Mercedes or fantasizing about revenge or glory. Insight isn't wish fulfillment. It is being the best version of yourself, making positive assumptions, and setting good intentions.

Part III of the Insight Cure is made up of the final two steps: reinforcing and living in your new reality. It's not enough to construct a new idea of who you are. You have to go into the world and experience being your new self.

Step seven: Testing the new story. Go into the world and test your new story to confirm and reinforce it. You'll start with small challenges with guaranteed successful outcomes. Then you'll level up to bigger challenges that will call upon your powers and strengths. Even if you fail, you still win, because every test gives you more insight into navigating life as a new person. Setbacks are setups for future success. As you accumulate experience, you'll settle into your new narrative and continually reinforce it until it starts to feel natural.

Step eight: Making change stick. By not acting out your former bad habits and destructive patterns, you allow the brain synapses associated with your old story to diminish and disappear. By acting on good habits and constructive patterns, you allow neurological pathways associated with your new narrative to form. Before long, your new habits and patterns will be normal and automatic. The old ones will feel strange and antithetical to your sense of self. In this step, you'll also learn resilience skills and how to use insight to get on track in case you find yourself sliding back.

By going through all the steps, gaining awareness and deep insight and reinforcing the new narrative until it becomes automatic, you will complete the process behind the Insight Cure and transform your life. You'll know, with confidence and clarity, who you really are and the amazing things you can do. To aid you on your path, I will provide many case studies of patients who have been through the Insight Cure and practical tools that will help you figure things out and become more self-aware at each step. I'll also check in with your emotions along the way so that you feel supported and capable of making the change you want.

The complete progression from step one to step eight will take between 6 and 18 months. It's a commitment. You've been operating under a false truth for a lifetime already, and excavating decades' worth of habits and patterns takes some doing. Your brain is plastic, meaning it can change, but it's not made of Play-Doh. Forging new neurological connections doesn't happen overnight. You have to live as a new person before you can *become* a new person. I promise that you'll feel steadily better and stronger as you progress, learn who you really are, and walk a different path through the world.

You Have the Power

The consensus among my colleagues in the field of psychology is that you need to see a therapist in an office setting to effect real change.

Respectfully, I disagree.

To a large extent, the prescription to see a therapist at least once a week for at least two years is self-serving and outdated. Once upon a time, you couldn't do anything without experts' input. But we live in the DIY age of information. Expertise has been democratized. If you wanted to, say, make a demo album, you used to have to go to a recording studio and work with a producer. Now you can teach yourself how to use GarageBand and record your own demo. To make a will or get a divorce, you once had to hire a lawyer to do the paperwork. Now you can go to LegalZoom.com and download the forms.

Not to say that you will never have to hire a lawyer—or a psychologist. If you are severely, acutely addicted, depressed, or anxious, with thoughts of suicide or self-harm, or if you suspect you have a disorder like bipolar or schizophrenia, you should seek help from a trained professional. But I believe the vast majority of people who want to improve the quality of their lives and relationships can make it happen without the inconvenience and expense of weekly therapy sessions. What they need is information, not doctors' bills. The stakes are high, and I don't take that lightly. This is your life, with your happiness and fulfillment on the line. By tackling your emotional issues, following the progression, and committing to the process, you will change your story and your life. And because you are doing it yourself, the benefits of the Insight Cure will be that much more meaningful to you. You are the cause and the effect. You already have everything you need inside you to be the person you want to become.

PART I

FIND
YOUR
TRUTH

Discover the false truth that is the root cause
of all your problems. What is your "story"?
Where does it come from?
How did this debilitating belief get started,
and how is it still defining your adulthood?

UNDERSTANDING WHY CHANGE IS HARD

When patients come to see me for the first time, they often bring in a list of the things they'd like to change. "My marriage is stale" or "I can't hold down a job," they say. And I tell them that these problems are symptoms, the result of inadvertent self-sabotage and the manifestation of a false truth, of some deep, elemental pain that is the root cause of all their suffering. Until they have reckoned with their false truth, they won't be able to make lasting, positive change.

I get a lot of side-eye when I explain that. Invariably, patients would rather talk about the symptoms, or the "what" (affairs, drinking, etc.), than the cause, or the "why" (the false truth).

The truth is, *what* people do isn't nearly as important as *why* they do it. And it's nearly impossible to change the *what*—the obvious problems and issues that need fixing—unless they know *why*. What's more, for most people *why* is a complete mystery. It does take some effort to solve the mystery of *why*. But by working together, we will solve it, and as a result, you will get unstuck from self-destructive patterns.

Whether you realize it or not, there are many *why* forces pulling the strings in your mind that you aren't even aware of. As you start this process, you'll learn how those forces originated and why they can make change difficult (but not impossible). Even the deepest roots can be uprooted.

Real change starts with self-awareness. In the Insight Cure, awareness isn't as simple as admitting you have a problem. It goes deeper. It's an understanding that a false truth exists, that it was formed long ago, and that it is entrenched in your mind. And most importantly, you need an awareness of the false truth itself. What is it? Where did it come from?

Often, people think awareness is all you need to change your life, but that is really only where you start. So let's begin at the beginning by figuring out what's *really* driving your behavior and making you do what you do.

Please remember that your desire to change is all the impetus you need to make it happen and see yourself successfully through this process. If you believe your life can be less of a struggle than it is now, that faith will eventually make a bright future your reality.

You Were Born to Change

Human beings have been evolving and adapting for millions of years. The mechanism that ensured our survival has been change. If we hadn't adapted to our environment, we would have died out tens of thousands of years ago.

As we evolved, our brains grew and our species learned. We went from living in trees and caves and being eaten by predators to dominating the planet. Our species' unique talent for adaptation exists within every individual person on earth. Striving to grow and learn is in our DNA. Humans are quite literally born to change. It's a mixed blessing. Along with our ability to adapt, we are also dogged by a relentless urge to keep evolving, no matter how successful we are as a species or as individuals.

Evolutionary psychology (EP), a relatively new domain, is the study of our elemental nature and how ancient motivators work in the context of modern life. EP derived from sociobiology, the founder of which was E. O. Wilson, my Harvard thesis advisor. I was a bio major interested in discovering the roots of behavior, and Wilson really was *the* man. Proving myself to him, a quiet and profound man with fatherly qualities, was an early attempt to feel more confident about myself and my own abilities. I learned that over the long haul, we must adapt or we will not survive. There's a basic truth to EP that we can all relate to, and I believe EP is an important merging of science and psychology and the study of human growth. It has identified 15 evolutionary motives—you could call them "primal urges"—that have motivated humans since caveman days, and continue to do so today.

THE FIFTEEN EVOLUTIONARY MOTIVES

1. **Lust.** Reproduction is the number one responsibility of any species. Today we have plenty of lust, along with birth control and courtship rituals.

2. **Hunger.** The urge to eat as much as possible whenever food is available saved cave dwellers during famines, but it's also why we have an obesity epidemic today.

3. **Comfort.** The motive for shelter once drove our ancestors to find a cave, build a fire, and sleep on moss. Now it's what drives our décor and real-estate obsessions.

4. **Fear.** Being afraid protects people from entering or remaining in dangerous situations, like putting ourselves in a position to be eaten by a bear or, today, walking down a dark alley in the middle of the night.

5. **Disgust.** Another protective motive, disgust kept cavemen from eating rotting food or wading into a bacteria-laden swamp. Now it drives us to stay sanitary.

6. **Attract.** Primitive people adorned themselves with jewelry, piercings, and body paint to attract a high-quality mate. Now we have makeup, fashion, hair stylists, and fad diets.

7. **Love.** Deep affection and a sense of responsibility for one another kept families together, then and now.

8. **Nurture.** The drive to care for, feed, and educate children is about the tribe's survival.

9. **Hoard.** Storing and amassing resources once protected people from scarcity and famine. Now hoarding is considered greedy or a sign of mental illness.

10. **Create.** Innovation—making a better spear, inventing the wheel—once aided in survival and now improves our daily lives.

11. **Affiliate.** The "fitting in" motive was about an individual figuring out how to contribute to the tribe. Now it's about finding a niche or people you can relate to.

12. **Status.** The higher your rank, the greater your resources and privileges. Modern society places intellect and skill over brawn (once you're out of high school).

13. **Justice.** Punishing or banishing wrongdoers protected the safety of the larger tribe. Now the law-and-order urge is the bedrock of a peaceful society.

14. **Curiosity.** The "What's out there?" motive is responsible for human expansion across continents and into space, be it actual or cyber. We are driven to explore.

15. **Play.** Humans practice survival skills by simulating them as a game—from rocking a baby doll to playing sports that mimic warfare.[1]

THE SHARP FOCUS: In the course of this book, you'll come upon paragraphs every so often called "The Sharp Focus," like this one, that narrow down the precise point I hope you will take away from the preceding section. This step is about *why*. There is no more basic form of motivation than primal urges. Do any of them resonate with you in particular? Be honest and pick a few that jump out as things that matter deeply to you. I've noticed in my practice that three or four resonate with individual patients, and that the ones they pick are not necessarily related. To uncover the mystery of your *why*, or false truth, clues can be found by narrowing down the things that you really care about. Don't worry about what your choices mean. At this stage, you're just gathering awareness, not analyzing what you discover.

FIRST IMPRESSIONS

Leo

When I first met Leo, 22, he complained about episodic bursts of anger. He would fly into a rage at his family and friends—and at himself—over relatively small incidents, and need days to recover before he could calm down.

"I don't think of myself as an angry person," he said despondently. "It's that no one really gets me, and it pisses me off, especially when I visit my parents. I always hope my father will say something about my career, but he never does." Instead of giving Leo recognition, his family is indifferent to his success, which makes him feel inadequate and insecure.

There's a lot going on in every reaction and situation that most of us are barely aware of. Smart and ambitious, Leo excelled at school and worked hard at jobs since he was a kid. But he never figured out how to relax and have fun (an imbalance in his *play* motive). His false truth seemed to be based on the idea that his family didn't think he had anything to offer (a flaw in his family's *affiliate* and *nurture* motives). Not receiving acknowledgment (a sensitivity to his *status* motive) confirmed his belief that he was worthless. This feeling set off a flood of insecurity that manifested itself as rage (really, the *fear* motive of fight-or-flight mode, expressed as "fight"), that drove him away from his tribe, a kind of wrongfully self-imposed *justice* motive.

Need Is a Powerful Motivator

Another way to look at why you do what you do is to view all actions through the lens of need, be it physical, emotional, mental, or spiritual.

In his 1954 book *Motivation and Personality*, psychologist Abraham Maslow organized human needs into a hierarchy, shaped like a pyramid, with the most basic human needs (air, water, food) at the bottom. If the lowest-level need is met, you can aspire to reach the next level, and so on, until you reach the very tippy-top of the pyramid of human needs.

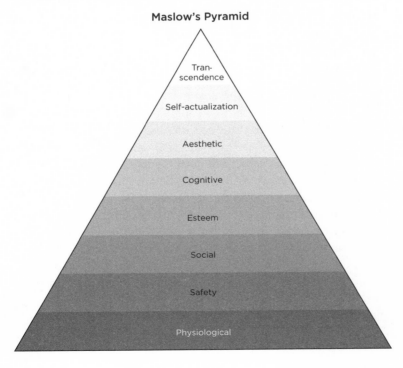

Maslow's Pyramid

The bottom four needs—physiological, safety, social, and esteem—are what Maslow called *basic* or *deficiency* needs, meaning if you are deficient in them, you can't move up to the top half of the pyramid. They are also defined as immediate short-term gratification needs that have to be fulfilled as soon as possible.

Physiological. Physiological needs include air, food, water, sleep, sex, and health. If you are starving and exposed, it's hard to aspire to anything other than survival.

Safety. Safety needs include a reliable income, safe shelter, accessibility to medical care, and living within a system that upholds laws and liberties and guarantees freedom from oppression. For example, Maslow might say that the entire population of North Korea is stuck at this level. If your safety is imperiled, the resulting stress and anxiety keeps you locked in, holding on to a job you hate or staying in a bad living situation.

Social. Social needs include the love and belonging of close family ties, trusted friendships, romantic intimacy, and positive interactions with others. If these needs aren't met, people feel alienated and isolated, which leads to depression and anxiety. Social needs drive people to stay in undermining friendships and unhappy or abusive marriages (or to have an affair). I know intelligent and attractive people who say, "I can't believe I'm single," and fail to realize their unstable careers and living situations might have something to do with that. Love is a need, but on Maslow's pyramid, safety comes first.

Esteem. Esteem means a need for acknowledgement of achievement from other people. We crave praise (like my patient Leo). We all know people who seem to have it all and post way too many photos on Facebook about their luxury vacations. When a person posts dozens of selfies in a day, I have to assume their esteem need isn't being met.

The next four levels are the *growth* or *being* needs, as in "being all you can be." Satisfy them to find long-term gratification, meaningful achievements, and authentic happiness.

Cognitive. Humans are born with the desire to learn and know things (the evolutionary *curiosity* and *creative* urges). If you have a big cognitive need, you probably watch the History

Channel, love to read, and lose whole afternoons falling down an Internet rabbit hole.

Aesthetic. This is the drive to seek out and appreciate beauty, balance, and symmetry in a human face and body, a flower, a cat, a painting, a building, the night sky, a Mozart symphony, or a Shakespeare sonnet. Not only do we need to look at and listen to lovely things, we also need to create beauty in our own art, style, fashion, and homes.

Self-actualization. Self-actualization is a bit more abstract. It is about needing to be more thoughtful, creative, peaceful, generous, and spontaneous, and living to our full potential. According to Maslow, only 10 percent of us reach this level. The other 90 percent are too wrapped up in lower-level needs like love, esteem, and safety.

Transcendence. A small subset of self-actualized people devote themselves to helping others with compassion, sympathy, empathy, and generosity. Only they reach the level of transcendence. Maslow put this at the very top because he believed that a life in service to others is the highest level of actualization. Wanting to help the less fortunate isn't enough. The transcendent have a selfless, virtuous heart and a *need* to do good.

THE SHARP FOCUS: The pyramid isn't an equation. It doesn't specify or measure the requirements for moving up to the next level. It is an interesting way of looking at your life and asking what's missing from it. I use the pyramid with patients to get them talking about what might be holding them back and what they need to push forward. If someone says, "I'm stuck at *esteem*," I wonder if their false truth has something to do with withholding parents. If someone says they're stuck at *social* or *love*, I wonder if childhood trauma affected their ability to trust in relationships. Like Maslow's hierarchy, the Insight Cure is a progression. You start with the basics and gradually move up in self-awareness.

Right now, ask yourself where on Maslow's pyramid you might be stuck. Look at the level above and the level below. Try to appreciate what being stuck where you are is all about. Consider the pyramid to be one more hint at what your *why* might be. You don't have to draw any conclusions yet. Just keep gathering those clues.

FIRST IMPRESSIONS

Daria

Daria, 26, a production designer in Los Angeles, was referred to me by her primary care physician. She was intensely frustrated by her interactions with other people, especially her parents and her twin sister. She said, "It's like I'm the only person who wants to talk about what's really going on. They just gloss over everything." Daria's twin sister's recent marriage had set off her anxieties. Since the engagement, she had felt a distance widening between herself and her previously inseparable sister. When Daria tried to talk to her family about it, she said, "They insisted I was wrong. I'm trying to be honest and keep it real. They refuse to go there. I can't stand the tyranny of bullshit!" She felt her parents saw her as desperate, needy, and troublesome. They reacted to her intensity by receding into reticence.

Growing up in San Francisco, Daria came from wealth. Her parents met every *physical* and *safety* need, but fell short on the next level, *social*. They were uncomfortable demonstrating closeness and intimacy, and whenever Daria asked for it, she was rebuffed. It felt like a betrayal to her every time. Her unmet social needs have caused problems in her nonfamily relationships as well. As a self-appointed "truth teller," Daria had a hard time making and keeping friends. When romances, friendships, and freelance jobs didn't work out, she didn't ask herself what went wrong. She put all the blame on the disappointing job or untrustworthy friend. Her false truth is something like "People always let me down." Despite her gifts of being energetic, intelligent, and attractive, she was stuck in deficiency needs, the bottom half of the pyramid.

The Identity Motive

Another way to understand your unique individual motivations for why you do what you do now is to examine how you have interacted with other people—successfully or unsuccessfully—in the past.

In the 1950s and '60s, German-born American social psychologist Erik Erikson developed the concept of *ego identity*, which is like an emotional fingerprint, a sense of self—whether strong or weak—that is unique to you. Your sense of self (ego) is honed through a lifetime of interactions with other people. As you mature, the lessons you learn at one developmental stage build on the previous stage. If you learn the necessary psychological skill associated with each stage, your sense of self, or your idea of who you are, gets a boost. I call these necessary skills "developmental gold," because they are the treasures you hopefully will discover in each stage and carry with you throughout your life. If you develop well, you'll probably make healthy, positive choices in life. However, if you don't learn what you need to, your sense of self takes a hit that knocks you out of a healthy emotional progression. Too many of those blows without catching up on emotional skills will make you more likely to make unhealthy, negative choices and have some emotional issues to deal with.

I've outlined Erikson's stages briefly below. (For more info, see page 235.)

ERIKSON'S STAGES

Stage One
Age: Birth to 1
Basic conflict: Trust versus mistrust
Successful development: A baby's adult caregivers feed him, keep him warm, dry, and safe, and give him the love he needs.
Ego identity boost: Security, trust in the world as a safe place
Unsuccessful development: A baby's caregivers are unreliable and/or inconsistent with feeding and nurturing.
Ego identity blow: Insecurity, feelings that the world is unpredictable and dangerous

Developmental gold: *Hope.* Even a well-cared for baby might feel let down by caregivers on occasion. He learns to hope for the best, with the understanding that it doesn't always happen.

FIRST IMPRESSIONS

Claudia

Claudia, 38, was referred to me by her music teacher when she told him she had distressing thoughts about harming herself. The artist-songwriter came into my office smartly dressed and acting highly competent and professional. I asked her why she was here, and she described feelings of near hopelessness. "No matter how hard I try, the world is invariably unfair," she said. She talked about caring for her mother throughout her terminal illness and how people praised her at her mother's funeral for all she'd done. "All I think about was how none of them cared as much as I did, including my sister." She seemed resentful of her uncomplicated, privileged life and didn't know why she wasn't tormented by hopelessness too. Gifted with fine organizational skills, Claudia often planned parties and special events for her friends. They loved her for it, but when she was at these parties, she felt little joy in her accomplishments. "It doesn't matter what I do. I never feel particularly happy about how it turns out," she said.

Claudia's predominant emotion of hopelessness made me think about her earliest stage of development. I wondered whether Claudia's caregivers had failed to instill trust in her when she was a baby or if something had interfered with her ability to hold on to this basic trust. In later sessions, we'd go deeper into her developmental history and I'd find out the truth.

Stage Two
Age: 1 to 3
Basic conflict: Autonomy versus shame and doubt
Successful development: A toddler learns to walk, talk, use the potty, and choose toys, clothes, and food, and is allowed to explore within safe limits.

Ego identity boost: Confidence, security, and control

Unsuccessful development: If a toddler's caregivers are controlling and overly cautious during emerging independence, she learns to be insecure and dependent. If a caregiver pushes a child to advance too quickly, she learns to feel inadequate and incapable.

Ego identity blow: Inadequacy, insecurity, dependence, and shame

Developmental gold: *Will.* A child encouraged to make choices and take control is free to call the shots in her own life—within reason.

Stage Three

Age: 3 to 5

Basic conflict: Initiative versus guilt

Successful development: A developmentally encouraged preschool child will assert his power by making up games and controlling play judiciously.

Ego identity boost: Courage, confidence, initiative, and creativity

Unsuccessful development: A criticized, discouraged child is afraid to initiate games, avoids other kids, and feels compounded insecurity about it. Guilt comes in when the parent or caregiver criticizes him for being a follower and not "getting in there."

Ego identity blow: Guilt, doubt, alienation, inadequacy, and inhibited creativity

Developmental gold: *Purpose.* Too much aggression isn't healthy either. Being a leader is good, but being a bully is awful. A well-adjusted child learns to lead some of the time and then allows others to take their turns.

Stage Four

Age: 5 to 11

Basic conflict: Industry versus inferiority

Successful development: School-age kids are put to work and put to the test. They receive grades and are judged by teachers and peers. If a child receives praise and encouragement, she'll learn to believe in her ability to get things done.

Ego identity boost: Pride and fortitude

Unsuccessful development: A child who never receives encouragement from teachers, peers, or parents is likely to disbelieve in her ability to get anything done.

Ego identity blow: Doubt and defeat

Developmental gold: *Competence.* Success requires a leap of faith that says, "I can do it." A well-developed school-age child might be intimidated by a task, but she'll tackle it anyway.

Stage Five
Age: 12 to 18
Basic conflict: Identity versus confusion

Successful development: The teenage years are about pushing boundaries and testing limits to develop a sense of self via trial and error. A teen explores different roles—sexually and occupationally—to see what fits, and examines his desires and interests under the (good or bad) influence of friends.

Ego identity boost: A strong sense of self

Unsuccessful development: Due to prior unhealthy development, the teen tries to figure out who he is, but the picture doesn't become clear, and he feels desperate, confused, worthless, and unhappy. He can't find a way to fit in.

Ego identity blow: An identity crisis

Developmental gold: *Fidelity.* A well-adjusted teen with a strong identity sees himself as part of a larger whole and likes participating in society so much that he's faithful to its established expectations and standards.

Stage Six
Age: 18 to 40
Basic conflict: Intimacy versus isolation

Successful development: With maturity comes a willingness to share one's strong identity and open one's heart to close, committed interpersonal connections and ultimately lasting, lifelong bonds.

Ego identity boost: Intimacy, fulfillment, and happiness

Unsuccessful development: If the young (and not so young) adult has a weak sense of self, she'll feel inhibited about opening up to others and forming close intimate relationships.

Ego identity blow: Isolation, loneliness, and depression

Developmental gold: *Love.* A meaningful, powerful connection to another human being that makes someone feel safe and happy in life.

Stage Seven

Age: 41 to 65

Basic conflict: Generativity versus stagnation

Successful development: A middle-aged person shifts from selfishness to selflessness, motivated to give back to society and family by helping the next generation. He looks back at the totality of his life as an individual and as a citizen of the world.

Ego identity boost: A strong sense of community, optimism, and expansiveness

Unsuccessful development: Driven by bitterness and disappointment, he doesn't feel motivated to give back or to see the bigger picture.

Ego identity blow: Isolation and a sense of aimlessness and purposelessness.

Developmental gold: *Care.* When a middle-ager feels proud of his accomplishments, he can shift his focus to caring for others as well as himself.

Stage Eight

Age: 65 to death

Basic conflict: Integrity versus despair

Successful development: A senior looks back at her life, accomplishments, and relationships with a sense of satisfaction. For the most part, she's made the right choices.

Ego identity boost: Integrity and strength

Unsuccessful development: A senior looks back with doubt, shame, guilt, and regret. She feels like her life was a waste of time.

Ego identity blow: Despair

Developmental gold: *Wisdom.* She appreciates life and accepts the inevitability of death.

THE SHARP FOCUS: I often use Erikson's stages in my practice to open up a discussion about when a patient believes things went off the rails. All too often, people go right to junior high, but that stage often shows us what are called *precipitating factors*, meaning that might be when you first noticed a problem, but it's not necessarily when it began. In my experience, *predisposing factors*, or when your life experiences initially conspired to create your false truth, occur much earlier. In search of *why*, really look hard at stages one through four. Do any of the ego blows catch your eye? Can you call to mind an event during that time in your life that was dominated by those negative feelings or beliefs? Take into account a *protective factor*, someone who provided a positive to offset a negative. A loving grandparent, supportive teacher, or good friend can give you enough confidence and support to develop healthily despite really awful parents or experiences. The power of a close, trusting relationship can't be underestimated.

Why Is Change So Hard?

If we are preprogrammed to desire change, are constantly trying to better ourselves, and can't help but learn and grow through our relationships and experiences, we have to wonder, "Why *don't* we?" Even if we have a deep desire to change, we still get stuck in our patterns, and change seems impossible.

Wanting to change

is human nature.

Getting stuck

is the human condition.

Change is hard because we tend to fear the unknown. A familiar but unhappy world is still known and therefore hard to abandon. Familiarity breeds complacency. Over a lifetime of thinking and behaving a certain way, people grow so accustomed to suffering that it feels normal, healthy, and "right." I can't tell you the number of times people have explained terrible choices and self-sabotaging behavior by saying, "It just felt *right*."

As you'll come to realize in the Insight Cure, "right" is often wrong.

Saying "It feels right" is just another way of saying "It feels familiar." Even if the emotional road is treacherous, at least you've been down it before. Our lives are far from perfect, but the accommodations are so profoundly familiar, we can't imagine living anywhere else.

Sigmund Freud wrote about "compromise formation." This is a big idea that helps explain a lot. When faced with a conflict between the way things could be and the way things are, people tend to seek a survivable compromise and to stay with it no matter how awful it is. Think about that: We adopt a compromise and stay with it even though it's not great or even what we really want. It's a survivable but flawed inferior posture with respect to the world. It holds us back from becoming our best selves, and it hurts.

Compromises form in a child's brain. Let's say a toddler draws a picture with crayons and is very proud of it. He's motivated by the *esteem* need to show it to a caregiver. If he doesn't get the reaction he hopes for, the discouragement might be so disturbing that he unconsciously compromises by not working as hard on his next drawing, not drawing at all, or not letting himself feel proud about future drawings. It might hurt at first to give up the pride and joy of drawing, but he'll quickly get used to repression. As he grows up, he might not know why he's embarrassed by praise or why he's disparaging of his own work and doesn't strive to realize his true potential. All he knows is that being judged—being noticed at all—is deeply uncomfortable.

Fear of the unknown and taking comfort in unhealthy familiarity and deeply embedded compromises are like heavy chains around your neck that you've been carrying for so long you don't even notice they're there. Some patients are aware of their chains when they start therapy, but most aren't. Nearly all of them have turned their chains into protection. They'd rather carry the burden than feel vulnerable without it. You know you're really ready to change when the burden becomes too great and too painful to carry any longer.

When people reach that point, they often seek help from others. Acknowledging that despite your best efforts, you can't reach your full potential on your own is an important step. We all need help in life, and I'm glad this book has found its way into your hands. I've put as much of my knowledge and experience as possible into it, and by reading it and working with the tools I've provided, you will be able to overcome lifelong hurdles, uproot deep compromises, and learn who you really are.

AWARENESS TOOL:

The Motivation Matrix

If you know why you do things, you can be smart about doing them the right way for the right reasons. To help you figure it out, Jim Taylor, Ph.D., a sports psychologist who has worked with Olympic and world-class athletes, has devised a "motivation matrix." It has two criteria:

Are you doing something because of internal or external influences?

Are you doing it for positive and healthy reasons or negative and unhealthy reasons?[2]

A blank motivation matrix looks like this:

	Positive and Healthy	Negative and Unhealthy
Internal Influences		
External Influences		

Next time you have a choice or a decision to make, try to see where it fits in this matrix. If your motivation to make positive changes comes from within, you're most likely to be successful. If you're motivated by external pressures and people, you might be able to make some changes, but they're likely to feel hollow and lead to dissatisfaction, burnout, and anxiety. Taylor has defined the likelihood of making real positive change based on which of the four quadrants your decision falls into.

	Positive and Healthy	Negative and Unhealthy
Internal Influences	You are motivated by desire, passion, gratification, validation, and satisfaction. If you set out to change for these reasons, you'll probably be successful, happy, and fulfilled.	You are motivated by fear of failure, inadequacy, and insecurity. If you set out to change for these reasons, you'll probably burnout, feel dissatisfied, and go back to previous bad behavior.
External Influences	You are motivated by recognition, status, money, and feeling superior. If you set out to change for these reasons, you might be successful, but you'll still rely on others opinions to feel good about yourself.	You are motivated by fear of loss, pressure from others, instability in life, and financial need. If you set out to change for these reasons, you might succeed, but you'll still feel anxiety and unhappiness.

Here's a filled-in matrix of the kind of things you might be saying to get yourself to make changes. Do any of the statements sound like you? See where your motivations fall in the matrix, and then go back to Taylor's predictions in the chart above to see how likely it is that your self-talk will lead to success.

	Positive and Healthy	Negative and Unhealthy
Internal Influences	"I want to lose weight and feel good about my body." "I'll tell my spouse the truth for a healthy relationship." "I want to work hard and do well for myself."	"I hate my body. I'm going to starve myself." "I'll lie to my spouse so I don't get in trouble." "I'll get a promotion, even if it kills me."
External	"I want to lose weight to be attractive for my partner." "I'll try counseling because my partner wants to." "My success will show haters how wrong they are."	"My partner said he'd leave me if I didn't lose weight." "I'll try a threesome because my partner wants to." "I hate my job, but my spouse will leave if I quit."

AWARENESS TOOL:

Problems Matrix

I often use another matrix for putting problems into perspective. The two questions I ask patients to think about are:

Is your attempt to solve the problem working or not working?

Is the problem fixable or not fixable?

Most often, it helps to make use of this matrix in order to locate the specific problem at hand and thereby determine its true nature. Then you can decide what to focus your efforts on.

	Fixable	Not Fixable
Working	Quadrant One	Quadrant Three
Not Working	Quadrant Two	Quadrant Four

All too often, we feel like our real dilemma is that too much of what troubles us is located in quadrant four: not working and not fixable. With the insight switch, you reconceptualize and refocus. What you often find is that the essential problem actually lies in quadrant two: not working but fixable. This is where the real action is, where real change needs to happen.

Make Conscious Change Happen

Having a conscious awareness of what's really motivating your behavior and actions is a huge help to the process of making positive change. It's like shining a spotlight on your behavior and gradually widening that beam so that eventually your motivations and choices are fully illuminated. You know who you are, why you do what you do, and how to make healthier decisions that lead to a happier life.

The work of this chapter is just opening your mind to the idea that something deep inside you, something you aren't yet aware of, is in control. The work of this book is taking control back. As you move through the Insight Cure, please:

Have faith. You might be thinking that you've been screwing up for a long, long time and that reading this book or doing these exercises isn't going to change anything. If I unburden you of the chains that weigh you down, what will you be left with? What will protect you? If you let go of your old ways, what will be the new way?

Trying a new way might cause an untethered feeling. I often compare it to being on a boat that's tied to an island pier. Cutting the ties and floating out into the ocean is terrifying. Most people say, "I'm going to stay right where I am, thanks." But boats are meant to be sailed. They're not supposed to be tied up. As much as the harbor looks like a safe place for the boat to remain, it's limiting and unhealthy. A boat left perpetually in a harbor will eventually rot and never reach its true potential and destination. Even if its destiny is to come back to the same port, it must undertake its journey. Merely staying is allowing your compromise formation to limit you forever.

Look at what you know for sure: You're unhappy and want to change. You know your life is problematic. You don't know what's out there beyond the horizon. It could be the same, worse, or much better. Have faith that there are better worlds to explore in the great unknown. If fear takes hold as you untie the boat, repeat the mantra, "I don't know what I don't know, and that's okay." By trusting in the process and the reality that you can have a different experience in life, you can overcome reluctance to cut yourself loose.

Have courage. Along with fear, there will be a bit of discomfort as you drift away from the familiar. Breaking away does include some pain. Before you feel much better, you'll feel a little bit worse. The relief at the end will be so profound, you won't care about what it took to get there.

The hardest, most painful step is the very first one. You might not feel ready to begin this journey. In AA they say, "It's harder to get stopped than to stay stopped"; here, the flip side is what's pertinent. It's harder to get going than to keep going. Take the step anyway. Waiting until you feel totally ready is the death of progress. Confidence is not required to begin. In fact, confidence is the pot of gold at the end.

When I was in graduate training in San Francisco, where we used a lot of Golden Gate Bridge analogies, a fabulous psychiatrist named Owen Renik said to me, "Look, if you have a patient who's standing on one side of the bridge and isn't able to cross, don't analyze why he can't cross. Help him take the first step with encouragement and support. You don't have to stand there and analyze why he's hesitant. Just get him moving. Do everything in your power to move him across the bridge, and then take a look back together from the other side and explore how come it seemed so difficult."

Reading this book is how you get moving. It's how you take that first step onto the bridge. You're sick and tired of complacency. There is a better life for you on the other side of the bridge. On a deep level, you know this is true. Even if you're scared, sad, and frustrated, use those emotions as the motivation to get moving.

Say, "By taking the first step, I begin the process of ending fear, sadness, and frustration." And then do it. Take the step, and just keep going.

Gut Check

At this stage of the journey, you might be feeling:

Anxious. Anxiety is nothing but fear of the unknown. Since you are leaving one world for another, you will face anxiety often as you progress. It's normal to feel worried about what you're about to do and to wonder how things will unfold.

Confused. "False truth"? "Unconscious narrative"? "Evolutionary psychology"? It's a lot to take in and digest. Some of the concepts might seem strange and illogical. It's only natural to feel a bit overwhelmed about all the information flowing your way. Don't try to become an expert. Just read the material and allow your mind to process it at its own pace.

Excited. You've been unhappy for a long time. These concepts ring a bell in your mind and you are feeling excited about finally making real change in your life. Good! It's motivating to feel psyched. Pace yourself, though. Take a deep breath and channel that eagerness into determination.

Skeptical. If you hear yourself thinking, "This is all bullshit!" I ask that you just bear with me for a little while. Open yourself up to the possibility that the science is real, the process works, and change can happen. When someone says to me, "What you see is what you get," I usually assume that their false truth is related to feeling fragile and exposed and they have developed an unconscious narrative of emotional stoicism in order to feel safe. Looking too closely at things equals vulnerability, and they'll do anything to avoid that.

Everything is revealing, no matter how a person tries to stay hidden.

There is always more to explore and become aware of. Your mind goes deep. Curiosity is a powerful tool, and the desire to learn more is only to your benefit. As I said at the beginning of this chapter, it's all about *why*. So ask yourself that question, and see what comes up. If (or, more likely, when) you reach a limit of your understanding, don't worry. More understanding, awareness, and insight may bubble up later, or we'll be able to detect or formulate it as you move through the process. Willfully suspend disbelief for the time being, and check in with your skepticism in a few chapters.

RECOGNIZING YOUR FALSE TRUTH

I can usually get a sense of a patient's false truth in the first therapy session. I look at how they frame their problems, their body language, the anecdotes they share. It's most often revealed in how they choose to present—to me and to themselves—and what they choose to conceal. After I've gotten to know a patient better over time, I can see the richer texture and complexities of their psyche. But during that first visit, a rudimentary picture of their fundamental problem takes shape in my mind.

How can I know so much about them within less than an hour of meeting them? We are all individuals with unique personal histories. Although they've been thinking about themselves for their whole lives, I have the training and objectivity to see them from the outside. I can follow the clues they're unconsciously sending me about the nature of their problem and how we can start fixing it. Their conscious mind says one thing. But the unconscious does all the deep communicating.

You've probably heard that human beings use only a small portion of their brains. Usually this is said in the context of extra-sensory perceptions. I'm not going to debate our dormant ability to bend spoons with our minds and other psychic powers. But exactly how much of our brains do we "use"? I can't say.

However, what I can say with confidence is that human beings *are aware* of only a fraction of our mental abilities.

The smartest person you know, someone who has read thousands of books and can hold forth on hundreds of subjects with intimidating intellectual prowess, only "knows" perhaps 10 percent of what's really going on in her head.

What's in the other 90 percent? It's a lot of automated stuff, unconscious life-preserving sensory-motor integration systems designed to make sense of our experience, keep us alive, and maintain the status quo without us even having to think about it. It's also a lot of long-term storage, a gelatinous warehouse of memories and emotions, some parts of which are easily accessible and available to be reconsidered and reworked while other parts have sturdy locks on the doors.

Insight is the key that unlocks those doors, giving you access to the hidden places in the mind and allowing you to overcome inertia. With those doors open, you can shine a light into the dark corners and illuminate the deeply buried or repressed memories that have made you who you are. With deep understanding about them, and with the proper guidance (for example, this very book), you can create the opportunity for the change you need and remake yourself into a healthier, more confident, and happier person.

This chapter shows you the lay of the land of your whole mind—the parts you know and the parts you aren't aware of yet—plus a few ideas about how to change your way of thinking (much of which is not actually conscious thought) to expose and recognize your false truth.

The Conscious versus the Unconscious Mind

The conscious mind is the headquarters of thought and includes executive functions like decision making, planning, analyzing, judgment, perception, and willpower. Your conscious mind is rational, not emotional. It is a thinker, not a creator.

The conscious mind's memory is short. It can recall the names of the people you're talking to or the address you're currently trying to reach, but not necessarily your own phone number or the names of the people you had a meeting with last week. Experts have determined that the short-term memory of your consciousness can hold only four thoughts at a time (or, as my yoga instructor would say, only one).[3] For example, say you are reading this book on the subway. Your conscious mind can simultaneously take in the words on the page, keep track of how many stops until your destination, know you're running late, and be offended by the person next to you who is wearing too much perfume—and that's it. Although you have many thousands of conscious thoughts per day, most of them are fleeting and pertain to identifying and classifying sensory input to interpret your immediate surroundings.

Conscious thought might be far-reaching, but it's not deep. You might be intellectually nimble and able to process information quickly and efficiently, including complex and difficult subject matter like trigonometry or Middle Eastern politics. But no matter how crammed with knowledge your conscious mind might be, it represents only the tip of the iceberg, the 10 percent above sea level, of your mental and emotional capacity. The vast reserve, much bigger and more powerful, is below the surface, where even the greatest intellectuals have little sway. This is what actually controls how you behave and react to life. People might think their conscious minds are in charge, but they'd be wrong.

In the 90 percent of your mind that is unconscious, a good amount pertains to your involuntary physiological functioning. For example, you don't consciously activate your adrenal gland to release cortisol when you're under stress. You don't consciously control the beating of your heart or the blinking of your eyelids. The unconscious does it automatically.

Conscious Mind vs. Unconscious Mind

The rest of the unconscious contains long-term memories—some painful, threatening ones that we willfully, deeply bury; some that we automatically and unconsciously repress—of everything that you've experienced since birth, plus emotions, intuition, fears, hopes, creativity, imagination, dreams, nightmares, habits, and patterns of thought and behavior. The billions of brain cells and trillions of neural synapses provide it with unlimited long-term memory storage capacity. Everything you feel, imagine, remember, and can't remember resides in the unconscious. You don't "know" what's in there. You probably don't "think" the contents of your unconscious affect your present conscious choices and actions. In fact, your unconscious "decides" nearly every choice, emotional reaction, and action you take.

For example, your conscious mind might think "I'm happy!" as you are walking down the boardwalk on a sunny summer day. But the emotion of happiness is not a conscious analytical thought. A memory has bubbled up from your unconscious that you may or may not be able to picture in your mind's eye, triggering an involuntary release of hormones that have locked into receptors in your brain, resulting in a feeling that your conscious mind determines to be happiness.

Or perhaps your conscious mind "knows" that being clingy or demanding has caused problems in past relationships, and yet you find yourself doing the same things in your current situation with full conscious awareness that it will drive your partner away. You watch yourself doing the wrong things, knowing it's a bad idea, but you feel compelled to do so anyway. Your conscious mind is the puppet; your unconscious mind is pulling the strings.

I believe it was Sigmund Freud who said that the unconscious life repeats itself. Insight comes when you convert unconscious to conscious. By making more of your mind "known" to yourself, you can break bad habits and change while still feeling safe and supported. You don't have to continue being a helpless puppet. You can live a happier life by understanding yourself and the world, testing the assumptions you make about things that happen and how you should react to them, and proving that you can do things differently. Insight gives you the strength you'll need. It allows you to take control of what you think and how you feel.

THE SHARP FOCUS: As you continue to gain awareness about your false truth, it's essential to accept that your unconscious mind exists and that it's big, powerful, and quite active. It's very difficult for people to understand that consciousness—what they know they know—is only a small portion of their mental life. Consciousness is logic, after all, and it seems illogical that most of what you do is a reaction to the powerful, domineering part of your mind that you aren't aware of. Just by acknowledging that you don't know everything, you become emotionally stronger. I've seen my patients struggle for control of their actions using willpower and logic and wind up making the same mistakes anyway. Just ask yourself, "Is it possible that my unconscious mind is controlling my behavior more than I realize?" Let the question sink in as you continue this chapter and the process of the Insight Cure.

Childhood Trauma

"It's a joy to be hidden, but a disaster not to be found," said Donald Woods Winnicott, a British psychoanalyst and the author of *Playing and Reality* (1971). I interpret his meaning to be that we all take comfort in our (hidden) false truth. You might not know what it is or how it came to be, but you've constructed a narrative for life around it and lived with it for a very long time. It's what you know. Winnicott's "joy" in being hidden refers to taking comfort in the familiar. But if you don't explore your unconscious and find out your false truth, you will stay the same and continue struggling. Or you can find your false truth, define yourself in a new and healthy way, be as happy as you deserve to be, and have a full life that includes helping others. Not reaching your true potential is Winnicott's "disaster."

This is really deep and profound. Let's take a little while to digest the impact of what we are dealing with here. You take comfort in the familiar. In living with your false truth, the world makes sense to you and you know what to expect. It's hard to imagine any other way. Yet there is so much more. You are like a little boat moored in a harbor. Remember the saying "any port in a storm"? But this port you've chosen is not a safe harbor. It is filled with falsehoods and contaminants. You have to get free to really live. Unmooring yourself and pointing toward the open sea can seem nearly impossibly daunting. But you are not safe in your harbor of false truth. You were made to head out into the sea of a broader awareness and a better life. The comfort of the familiar must go. You must go on to be found, to find your real truth and the strength and joy that is within you.

As I mentioned before, the conscious mind is the tip of the iceberg, and the unconscious is the submerged bulk. I think of the separation between the unconscious and the conscious as a porous membrane, allowing feelings and memories from the depths to pass into interpretive thought. The membrane is most permeable when the conscious mind is resting or when you're tired, dreaming, under hypnosis, extremely relaxed in meditation or prayer, on certain drugs, or in a coma. Interestingly, during those permeable states of consciousness, you are at your most creative. This makes sense, since imagination exists in the unconscious.

To gain insight, you have to drift down into your unconscious to find flashes of memories, feelings, and thoughts about a trauma that was disturbing to you as a child.

What constitutes a "trauma"?

A trauma doesn't have to be a major event. It could be a seemingly small incident that you took deeply to heart. A misunderstanding or an insult or emotional injury that, in a child's mind, got blown out of proportion. Some experts use the word *microtrauma* for these small, seemingly innocuous disturbances that take root and grow into something bigger in the mind. A series of microtraumas, when the same insult or injury happens over and over again, compounds the impact.

A major trauma is otherwise known as an adverse childhood experience (ACE). ACEs have been proven to be so harmful to a child's brain that they increase the likelihood of chronic disease, mental illness, violent behavior, and revictimization decades later. In the landmark 1998 study by researchers at the Centers for Disease Control and Kaiser Permanente, ten ACEs were measured among 17,000 subjects.[4] These ACEs were:

- physical abuse;
- emotional abuse;
- sexual abuse;
- physical neglect;
- emotional neglect;

- having a depressed or mentally ill parent or household member;

- having an alcoholic or addicted parent or household member;

- having an imprisoned parent or relative;

- witnessing physical abuse of a parent; and

- losing a parent by death, divorce, or separation.

According to the study's findings, 64 percent of the racially and economically diverse adult subjects had at least one of these ACEs (there are other ACEs, of course, like bullying, that were not measured in this study). If a person had one ACE, they were 87 percent likely to have had two or more.

You can calculate your own ACE score by adding up the types of trauma you've experienced. Count per ACE, not per specific incident; so if you were emotionally abused one time or daily, it's one point. The higher your score, the greater your risk for every negative adult outcome, from being a smoker or an alcoholic, to being depressed or anxious, to getting fired or divorced, to being a violent criminal or the victim of violence. People with an ACE score of six or more are likely to have their life span shortened by 20 years compared to less traumatized people.

Recent health-care programs in at-risk communities such as prisons and tribal areas have found that when people are made aware of the research that ACEs often lead to bad behavior as an adult, it helps them change their course and get on a healthier, happier track. As the original study leader, Robert Anda, recently told the *New York Times*, "In my experience people who have experienced a lot of ACEs don't put it all together for themselves. [Once they do] they have an opportunity to understand their own lives better and they can change."[5]

THE SHARP FOCUS: Whether your trauma was a case of misunderstanding or an even greater adverse experience, gaining awareness and then insight into what happened is the only way to heal and be the person you want to become. Really, you *have* to deal with it, and that usually means out loud, either by talking it through with a therapist and/or sharing part of your experience with at least one other person in your life whom you know you can trust. Awareness of having lived through a trauma or traumas—micro or otherwise—in itself is not enough to free you from the pain of your present existence or from negative expectations and bad patterns of behavior. For real change, you need a deeper appreciation of the operational emotional dynamic—the real push and pull of feeling as you reacted to the events themselves and what you expected of yourself and of others on a gut-feeling level.

FIRST IMPRESSIONS

Skylar

Several years ago, Skylar, 24, was referred to me by her father to discuss some "issues" she faced. At that time, she was suffering from bulimia, living in Los Angeles, taking acting classes, and looking to find her voice and sense of purpose.

Skylar was smart, articulate, and forthcoming. In our first session, she admitted that she supported herself by working as an escort with an agency focused on arranging "dates" between older, successful men and younger women. I asked her, as I always do, to tell me about her experience growing up.

"I grew up [on the East Coast] in a loving home. I was the only child and my parents were very good to me. I'm not sure it's connected to the bulimia, but my grandfather sexually molested me for a while."

She told me this matter-of-factly, and I wondered if she'd shared the fact that she'd been abused with other people. It turned out that she hadn't spoken about it, either with her conservative parents or with her friends. Her coolness in reporting it to me made me wonder if her false truth had to do with the belief that she caused the abuse or deserved it somehow. I assured her that her childhood abuse was absolutely connected to her eating disorder, her choice of employment, and other problems she might be having. Skylar nodded, but seemed doubtful. "I didn't let it get to me," she said. The abuse happened from the time she was 9 until she was 12.

In our early sessions, we tried to trace the consequences of the abuse in her life experience. In school, she felt isolated and alone. "The other kids were afraid of me. I guess I came on more sexual than anyone else, starting early, in junior high. I dressed in short skirts and tight tops. I was sexually free and they were all repressed." Skylar made a name for herself as more than a little exhibitionistic. If she felt judged by her peers, she said, "I judged them right back. They were all losers and idiots. I had a few close friends, but I kept my distance from everyone else."

Feeling isolated and being overly sexualized are common traits of victims of childhood sexual abuse. Her eating disorder was a manifestation of feeling out of control. But I didn't think her false truth was "It's all my fault," as it is for many victims. It seemed to come up over and over again that the men (and the women) she met were all horrible people, deserving her scorn. I formulated that her false truth was *"Everybody* is some kind of creep, and *no one* should be trusted."

Her father had been emphatic that she come to therapy, but she didn't want to. "I don't see why I'm here. There's no work to be done. I'm fine," she insisted.

"But what about your bulimia symptoms?" I countered, caringly. "These problems don't take care of themselves."

"I'll have to work something out," she said.

"We'll have to work something *through,*" I reframed.

The biggest hurdle for the first two months of sessions was to get Skylar to trust that it was safe for her to go deeper with me and explore the emotional connections between her past, her beliefs about what to expect, and the present. Through constant caring and purpose, I had to prove to her that she could feel safe with me.

The Hidden Truth

Many of my patients come into therapy with a hundred stories about things that have happened in their lives that they believe are the causes of their unhappiness. But when I tell them that all of these stories derive from one original false truth or one painful reaction to a forgotten experience, they don't believe it. "My childhood was fine," they often reply. "Nothing bad happened."

I can say for sure that something most definitely *did* happen to each one of us. Children see things from a very narrow perspective: Am I safe? Do I feel secure? Do the people in charge of my survival care about me? Children lack the experience, understanding of nuance, and perspective to put parental actions and words into a larger context. Without context, even loving parents' behavior can be unsettling to children.

Whatever it was, the trauma or series of microtraumas you experienced unleashed unsettling feelings that caused you to make an adjustment in your behavior or thoughts to cope with the troubling emotions. Although the adjustment made you feel better at the time by giving you a sense of safety and control, in the long run it twisted your sense of self and your place in the family and the world. It became your default setting, your fallback reaction to life's challenges. Whenever you're upset, your false truth is reactivated. It runs so deep that it has shaped your psychology and established patterns of behavior that continue to define you as an adult. Every person has a unique false truth, "pathogenic belief," or "maladaptive belief" based on their unique childhood experience. Siblings from the same home can have completely different false truths.

How does a traumatic event turn into a false truth and then into a maladaptation?

- A child whose mother is anxious and overly protective might develop the false truth that his own independence is dangerous. When he starts to feed himself, crawl, or walk, his mother gets upset and nervous. She's responsible for his survival, so if she's upset, he becomes frightened. The false truth "Success is dangerous; failure is safe" takes root. He adjusts his behavior to be incompetent and dependent, creating the unconscious narrative, "When I get close to success, I have to pull back immediately." As an adult, the person who unconsciously fears success will sabotage his relationships and career to confirm his false truth. He has no idea why he's wrecking himself.

- A child whose parents fight all the time might develop the pathogenic belief that he's to blame for the fighting. It feels safer to be the cause than to accept that the fighting is completely unpredictable. His false truth is "Everything's my fault." He might maladapt by being obsessively careful. His unconscious narrative could be, "If I'm not perfect and super careful, all hell will break loose." The perfectionist will become a chronically insecure egomaniac who is inappropriately devastated when small things go wrong.

- A child whose parent criticizes her for crying might develop the pathogenic belief that overt expression is disturbing for others and therefore dangerous for her. Her false truth is "Expressing myself is bad." She'll maladapt by suppressing negative emotions in order to be a "good girl." Her unconscious narrative becomes, "If I let people know what I'm really feeling, they'll reject me." The bottled-up person's fear of vulnerability will prevent her from developing deep and intimate relationships or taking necessary risks in her career. She's likely to seek out overly dramatic, troubled people who confirm her unconscious belief that being expressive leads to suffering.

- A child whose parents are depressed or deprive themselves might feel like she's betraying her parents by being happy or indulging herself. This feeling of disloyalty when doing something that conflicts with her parents' preferences might lead her to deny herself even if she wants to enjoy an experience or achievement. Her false truth would be "I can't let myself be happy or I'll feel bad." So she makes sure that her success, if she allows herself to have it, is a secret shame or guilt. She feels as if she's taking too big a piece of the happiness pie for herself and leaving loved ones to do without.

It's a cliché about therapy that doctors blame the parents for everything. Unfortunately, there's some truth to that. Even if parents are loving and have the best intentions, they still mess up their kids. If it's not the parents, it's the grandparents, or the siblings, or the racist, sexist culture we live in. Pathogenic beliefs are born of children's limited capacity to understand adult behavior and society. They're just kids! They don't know any better. The tragedy is that as adults, the unconscious narrative from childhood keeps throbbing away in their psyche but outside their awareness, framing their outlook on life and constructing a set of expectations about who they are and how life should be.

Of course, some parents are *not* loving, and they deserve blame. They can do serious harm to their children's brains, along with their minds. Brain development is actually the process of turning physiological and emotional input into neurological connections, called synapses. Many of these connections created by physiological and emotional input are found in the prefrontal cortex, the social region of the brain, which governs emotion, empathy, and interpersonal signals. These connections are like wires that light up in response to stimulation. If you do or feel something a few times, synapses are created. If you do or feel it repeatedly, those neural pathways are strengthened and deeply embedded.

Sue Gerhardt, psychotherapist and author of *Why Love Matters: How Affection Shapes a Baby's Brain*, wrote, "The social brain develops in response to the social experiences that a baby actually has. Neural pathways get laid down as a result of actual experiences. . . . In the second and third years of childhood, that huge tangled mass of connections starts to get 'pruned'—on a 'use it or lose it' basis. Basically, we keep the pathways that are most used and most useful in our particular social environment—and lose those pathways that have not been used that much. That means that if as babies and young children we live with angry, aggressive people, we will keep pathways that help us to be alert to anger and aggression, and if we live with people who are attentive to other people, we will keep the pathways that help us to be attentive."[6]

If a child lives under constant threat, his brain is steeped in so much cortisol (the fight-or-flight hormone) that anxiety and stress are all he perceives. "When babies are chronically stressed, this can create permanent damage to their systems and they grow into adults who are not able to recover quickly from stressful events," wrote Gerhardt. "They become more vulnerable and sensitive to stress as adults." It gets worse: An excess of cortisol makes it impossible for the brain to uptake serotonin (the happy hormone). The chronically stressed child's brain's natural soothing system is damaged. Adults who as children were wired for stress can't calm themselves down. They often have anxiety disorders, depression, aggressive personalities, behavioral problems, and addictions.

FIRST IMPRESSIONS

Steve

Newly separated at 52, Steve came to see me at the insistence of his extended family. He'd had orthopedic surgery and got a sizable prescription for oxycodone, which turned into an opioid addiction. "It smooths things over real nice," he said. "The only thing that ever has." Steve described a lifetime of self-medication to deal with stress, using alcohol and pot as well as Valium and quaaludes. He had a mild form of ADHD that went undiagnosed and untreated for years. He also described one episode of childhood molestation by older classmates when he was eight. I asked about his marriage, and he seemed strangely calm about the separation. "She had enough of me," he said. "I can't say I blame her." The entire session, Steve acted superficially cheerful and amped up and said things that seemed intended to shock, like "Every day is great until it comes time to blow your brains out." In our first session, we barely scratched the surface of his history of ACEs. I suspected Steve's neural pathways were wired for stress. Substance abuse and acting out often are predictable symptoms of this sort of brain wiring.

Unconscious Habits and Behaviors

To change your life, you have to recognize the old "story" from childhood. Once you have uncovered your false truth's origins and eradicated the unconscious narrative that's been holding you back, the next step is to use insight and self-knowledge to write a new, *conscious* narrative, one that is designed for confidence and capability in every realm. By living with the new narrative, you'll make healthy choices that will eventually become automatic and permanent.

> ALTHOUGH THE OLD NARRATIVE
> WAS "WRITTEN" IN CHILDHOOD,
> IT'S NOT WRITTEN IN STONE.

So what do you do? First, recognize your false truth. Start by examining your life today for patterns and reactions. In psychological terms, patterns are thoughts, habits, or actions you repeat over and over and over again. You might be aware that they exist and be desperate to change them. You might think you can do it on willpower or desire alone.

To change these patterns of behavior, you have to recognize them for what they are: the manifestations of your false truth; the externalization of your inner reality; and unconscious thoughts that become negative outcomes.

A friend of mine is well educated and eminently qualified for senior positions in technology, but he has had a pattern of losing jobs because of his temper. He becomes furious when he's criticized. For a while, he bottles up the anger until the day he explodes at a colleague, an underling, and sometimes the boss. Then he's promptly fired. My friend acknowledges his anger-management problem and has tried various cognitive behavioral strategies, like breathing exercises, to keep his rage under control.

Unfortunately, acknowledgment isn't enough. He needs insight into the unconscious story in his head that triggers his rages. Counting his breaths will help tamp down his episodes temporarily, but they won't stop him from repeating this pattern of self-sabotage.

After many discussions in a nontherapeutic context (he was a friend, not a patient), he shared that his parents—immigrants who were desperate to assimilate and driven to present themselves and their children in the best possible light—set high expectations for his success from a very young age. "I don't remember it, but my mom told me this story," he said. "I took my first steps and got halfway across the room. My parents applauded and told me to try again, to get all the way across the room. My father held out a piece of chocolate as a bribe. Every step I took toward him, he took another step back. If I fell down or cried in frustration, he told me I couldn't have the chocolate. When I pushed myself, he gave me the candy. My parents trained me like a dog." His false truth was that compliance equaled love and that failure was unforgivable. From there, he grew up believing that "Only complete victory is acceptable." Whenever he made errors, he felt unworthy. At work, he unconsciously forced his bosses to fire him for making mistakes. His rages were directed at others, but he was really angry at himself for not getting the adult version of chocolate (praise and promotion).

RECOGNIZING PATTERNS

Larry

In my early sessions with Larry, 62, a serial adulterer, certain patterns emerged. His girlfriends were all assistants and secretaries, young women who looked up to him.

I asked about his life growing up. "My father gave in to my mother about everything, including how to raise me," he said. "She was tough on me about grades and chores. If I got one B, she'd scream and ground me. I rebelled against her by sneaking out of the house at night. When she caught me, I kind of liked it. I had showed her I could assert myself." The defensive, rebellious boy had grown into a successful man, married to an even more successful and quite famous wife.

"I don't know why I cheat," he said. "Aren't all affairs about conquest and the fear of death?"

His lovers weren't just younger. They were far less educated and accomplished than he was. I suspected Larry chose them to rebel against the authority of his wife, as he had with his mother. Or, by choosing women who were inferior to his wife, he was confirming his deep insecurity and sense of unworthiness put in place by his critical mother and neglectful father. Larry seemed to think his girlfriends gave him an ego boost. But actually, his affairs probably made him feel worse about himself.

Through our discussion, he saw that his wife had become an emotional stand-in for his mother. "My wife is the opposite of my mother, personality-wise. She's kind and patient. My mother was a real hard-ass. But my wife does manage to get her way all the time."

I asked about his father's role in his childhood.

"He just did whatever my mother said," Larry told me. As he spoke he recognized a similar dynamic between his mother and father as between himself and his wife. Larry's patterns of behavior were clearly linked to his past, his parents' marriage, and the as-yet-undiscovered false truth from childhood. I suspected it was about feeling like he'd never measure up and that being punished was better than being ignored.

Open Your Mind's Ear

Only the most insightful among us can begin to describe our interior monologues. Most people can't hear their own thoughts, especially not the false truths from childhood that have played on a loop, hundreds of times a day, for decades. Our "inner basis" (how we experience life inside our head) is like a white-noise machine, making fuzzy sounds that we don't consciously hear. But we do unconsciously hear them, react to them, and live by them all the time.

Training yourself to tune in to your interior monologue, a big part of my process, can bring about insight. I worked with a young woman in her early thirties with a compulsive eating disorder. Her weight had fluctuated up and down within a 40-pound range since junior high. She was all too aware of her weight fixation and her habitual, self-destructive diet-binge-repeat behavior pattern, but she was powerless to stop. She was in terrible pain and needed immediate relief.

Thinking of a cognitive behavioral technique, I urged her to buy a "clicker," the kind of counting device you can get at any sports supply store, to carry in her hand and click every time she had a negative thought about weight, body image, food, or eating. She counted over 200 hateful thoughts on her first day. "I had no idea how bad it was," she said. "A horrible thought came into my mind every few minutes." While tuning in to her interior monologue, she realized some of her thoughts were things her fat-phobic mother had said to her verbatim since she was a kid.

This observation was a crack of light that would soon enough flood her psyche with the illumination of insight. We had a lot of work to do to get to the bottom of her false truth, and awareness was the necessary first step.

AWARENESS TOOL:

Listen to Your Unconscious

Your unconscious can reveal itself in your spoken language, so train yourself to listen to the words that are coming out of your mouth, especially the specific phrases you use to describe yourself. Twice a week, use a voice memo app or recorder, and record yourself completing the following sentences:

"I always_____."

"I never_____."

"I can't_____."

"I can_____."

Start with the first prompt and repeat it until you come up blank with ways to finish it. Let the words and thoughts stream. Don't think about what they mean or whether you actually agree with what you say. Just speak. If it helps, close your eyes and do your recordings when you're a little tired. Your sentences might be mundane, like "I always cross at the light" or "I can run a mile in seven minutes," or emotionally profound, like "I never get what I want" or "I can't do anything right." Over the next few days, whenever you hear yourself using these opening phrases in conversation or as private thoughts, make a note or recording of where you were, what you were doing, and what you were referring to.

Always, *never*, *can*, and *can't* are very powerful words. They create dangerous generalizations about who you are. Sweeping generalizations cause prejudice about racial and religious groups. And you might realize how profoundly you are forming prejudices about yourself. By doing this exercise, you'll hear your unconscious pigeonholing and be able to cut it off. When these mischaracterizations stop, you can begin to figure out who you really are and what you really can (and can't) do.

The Power of Expectations

Expectations create reality. Your assumptions about life are embedded in your unconscious, often based on your false truth. Since childhood you've developed a set of anticipatory ideas about how things are supposed to unfold. You've confirmed those (generally incorrect) assumptions by behaving in a certain way to guarantee the anticipated (if unfortunate) result. Your unconscious controls your behavior to make sure things go as expected.

ASSUMPTIONS ABOUT LIFE
BECOME YOUR LIFE.

The phrase *anticipatory ideas* comes from control mastery theory (CMT), a domain of psychology that has been around since the 1950s, and pertains to the idea of the formation of a pathogenic belief in childhood that has given you a predictive understanding of the world. What you assume will happen happens. A little kid whose parents look the other way when she does something she's proud of will develop the anticipatory idea, "No one cares, and if I try to get their attention, I'll just be disappointed." In adulthood, this might manifest as a person who assumes attracting any kind of attention—at work or from a mate—is a losing proposition, and then she will make it so.

If you assume the world is indifferent or hostile, you are probably bitter and defeated. If you assume the world is caring and basically good, you are probably happy and optimistic, and walk through life with confidence, your arms open to receive and give love.

Most of us are very attached to what we think is going to happen. If things go exactly as you expected on a first date or a job interview, it's because your unconscious loves to be right. One way we can be right is to make sure things go wrong, as in "I *knew* this was a mistake!" or "I *knew* I'd blow it!" It's human nature to confirm your beliefs, even if they are wrong and hurtful.

Anticipatory ideas are an excellent "tell" for your false truth. How did your expectations come about? What childhood experience created them? Simply acknowledging that they exist is a giant step toward unburdening yourself of them.

QUIZ:

Anticipation Is Making Me . . . *What*?

For the following questions, choose the answer that best reflects how you believe you'd handle each situation.

1. You are going on a blind date, meeting at a restaurant for dinner. How will he or she react when you sit down at the table?

    a. He or she will look at you with disappointment, make an excuse, and leave.

    b. He or she might seem game at first, but will eventually lose interest. There won't be a second date.

    c. He or she will like how you look and be fascinated by your personality. It'll be a great night that will lead to other great nights.

    d. Who cares what he or she thinks? You'll probably be turned off and will make your own excuses to get out of there.

2. You're about to give a big presentation at work. How do you think it'll be received?

    a. Despite all your preparation, you'll choke when you get up in front of the room. You won't be able to handle the pressure.

    b. You'll get up there and do your thing, but your audience will zone out or check their phones throughout the presentation.

    c. You'll nail it. Excellent preparation, brilliant delivery. They'll love you.

    d. You'll be great, but your audience is just too stupid to appreciate your ideas.

3. You are driving on the highway. A reckless driver cuts you off and nearly causes an accident. You give him a loud honk. What happens next?

    a.   You pull over, shaken, hoping that the driver doesn't pull over too and start a fight.

    b.   You drive away, furious at the driver and at yourself for being afraid to challenge him face-to-face.

    c.   You have the presence of mind to write down the driver's license plate number and call the cops.

    d.   You chase him down and release your road rage on him.

4. You and your partner just had a huge fight. Where will you be 15 minutes from now?

    a.   Alone in the bathroom with the door locked.

    b.   Alone in the bedroom, steaming mad and pretending to watch TV.

    c.   Sitting at the kitchen table across from him or her as you talk it out calmly and rationally.

    d.   At the bar, on your second drink.

5. You are going to a party thrown by an acquaintance. You might not know many people. How long will you stay?

    a.   Ten minutes, long enough to say hi to the host.

    b.   Twenty minutes, long enough to say hi to the host and make one round.

    c.   A couple of hours. So many new people to meet and get to know.

    d.   Zero minutes. Why bother going? You'd rather stay home.

Scoring

Actually, there is no scoring for this quiz. Any answer besides "I don't know" proves that you have a strong set of anticipatory ideas. You think something will go a certain way, and more often than not it does, which is proof of only one thing: **expectation is a self-fulfilling prophecy.**

Explore the Possibilities

With patients, I work to undo expectations by discussing them. You don't know what's going to happen when you walk out the door. Anything could take place, good or bad. If you "know" the outcome before it happens, you're cutting off a huge number of unexpected possibilities.

The influential and enigmatic family systems therapist Salvador Minuchin used to want to see everybody in the household all at once. Even pets came to the session. He was fascinated to learn how everything affected everyone. He saw patterns, of course, and he loved to make sense of the operating dynamics. Early in my career, I remember discussing a complicated situation with him and asking for his advice. He suggested, "Well, tell everyone just to do something different for a change."

"Huh?"

He clarified, "Since you don't know what to recommend, let's at least introduce some new dynamics. That way they'll see more clearly how old dynamics play out. They'll reform very quickly when they see that."

This is true for groups and this is also true for individuals. Are you not sure what to do but want to explore different possibilities and learn more about what you customarily unconsciously or consciously seek or set up? Take a different approach. Act differently than usual. See what happens.

An exercise I do with patients is to have them use their imagination (thereby accessing the unconscious) to come up with a dozen potential outcomes for any situation that is causing them anxiety. I ask the patient to suggest a few positive potential outcomes and a few negative ones, a few that are banal, a few that are completely outlandish. We discuss how it would feel to go into a situation without any expectations at all. They usually say, "Nerve-racking."

People don't realize how impactful their attitude about life can be on their actual existence. In fact, people often don't know what their attitude about life *is*. By asking them to define it in words and phrases, I can catch a glimmer of insight almost immediately.

When I'm getting to know a new a patient, I ask, "Where are we starting from? What are your assumptions about life?"

The question seems straightforward, but it's actually arresting. Patients are perplexed, and intrigued, by it. They tend to pause and say, "Let me think about that for a minute." They might not have an answer on the tip of their tongue, but if they start talking and formulate a response, it can be intensely significant.

Consider the range:

Pessimistic: "Life sucks and then you die."

Optimistic: "Love is sustaining."

Nihilistic: "Life is meaningless."

Pragmatic (á la Winston Churchill): "Success is not final. Failure is not fatal. It is the courage to continue that counts."

Once, I asked a new patient, "Tell me about yourself. Who are you?"

The middle-aged man responded, "I'm a successful surgeon."

"So you're saying your work defines you."

The man looked shocked for a second, and then started laughing and nodding with recognition. "What's it like for you to know people better than they know themselves?" he said.

The truth is, I don't understand him or anyone better than they do. I can only point people in the right direction to discover themselves. I responded to his comment by saying, "Let's keep going. Let's take a closer look at what that's about."

Take a closer look at your attitude about life. Dig into a memory or emotion from your unconscious that sheds light on how you came to feel this way. There are no right or wrong answers. There's only exploration and discovery. Your goal isn't correction (not yet). It's only learning about yourself and making connections between what you think and how you act.

Take a few minutes to compose an attitude about the life you want. How do you see your existence? How do you aspire to live? **Right now, without too much conscious thought, describe an aspirational assumption about your new life in just a few sentences.**

_____

_____

_____

_____

AWARENESS TOOL:

The Ping Test

Powerful feelings of deep shame, guilt, submission, depression, or fear formed in your unconscious when you were very young, and have since developed into toxic patterns of thought and behavior in adulthood. To change your life, you have to recognize the false truth that is controlling you. Some common ones I see all the time in my practice are the following:

"I'm no good."

"I'm bad luck."

"No one likes/loves me."

"No one gets me."

"I'm toxic."

"I'll always be alone."

"I'm unlovable."

"I'm a liar."

"I'm a fraud."

"I'm totally superficial."

"I'm a loser."

"I can't get anything right."

"I'm a cruel person."

"I just don't care."

"I can't succeed."

"I can't excel."

"I'll never get what I deserve."

"I don't deserve to be happy."

"My feelings don't matter."

"I can't show my feelings."

Do any of these toxic narratives ping your radar? Do any of these examples resonate deeply in your gut? Have they been playing on a loop in your mind since childhood—in some cases, since before memory or speech—and reinforced unconsciously in your actions and choices?

Circle the phrases above that resonate with you. Compare them to other clues you've gathered in this chapter—obvious patterns of behavior and thought, dangerous generalizations you've made about yourself, your assumptions about life—and you can probably recognize your false truth. If you feel like you have a good idea of what it is, write it down.

My false truth is _____

_____

_____

If you don't feel confident enough to "declare" a false truth, that's absolutely fine! Perhaps all you can do at this point is acknowledge that your unconscious exists and that there's more in your head than you previously realized.

You've been gathering clues for two chapters now. Take all of them with you into the next chapter, where we'll go even deeper into the unconscious and try to pin down exactly when, and how, the false truth came to be.

Gut Check

While acknowledging that you experienced a childhood trauma and trying to understand how it affected you, you might feel:

Confused. The false truth as a concept might be hard to grasp. If you're completely baffled, try rereading the chapter. The Insight Cure process is about discovering and eradicating the false truth, so it is important that you understand the basic idea: Something happened that made you see yourself in a certain way, but as a kid, you were wrong about how you interpreted things. The false truth is that misinterpretation. The unconscious narrative is how you changed yourself or maladapted to the false truth to feel better without knowing you were doing it (hence making it unconscious).

Doubtful. Perhaps you're thinking, "Really, a 'maladaptive belief' from childhood has a profound impact on problems in adulthood?" It's understandable to have doubts about the very concept. I'll ask you to trust in the decades of science behind this process and just live it as if it were real, despite skepticism, for the time being.

Relieved. As ACE studies have revealed, just knowing that trauma from childhood is to blame for problems in adulthood gives people a sense of relief. The person is not the problem. The problem is the problem. Acknowledging that they were damaged in the past lifts a lot of shame and guilt off people's shoulders. Awareness starts healing.

Resentful. Many patients react to these concepts with resentment. Their parents really messed them up. Even though they left home behind, the damage of childhood casts a long shadow to this day. In upcoming chapters, you'll learn to manage resentment and other negative emotions. For now, allow emotions to surface. Everything you feel is relevant to this process. As you learn more about interpreting your experiences, you'll gain insights through them. Try to be open to whatever comes up.

TRACING THE FALSE TRUTH'S ORIGINS

Your false truth came to be at a moment in time, in the aftermath of a trauma or a series of microtraumas. Your earliest ideas about who you are and how you fit into your family—and, by extension, the world—were formulated at that time. As this concept of yourself took root, it developed into the unconscious narrative that still controls your behavior and thoughts to this day.

What are the origins of your false truth? What happened? Where did it happen? Who was there?

The details of your false truth's origin are important. They provide the missing puzzle pieces in the big picture of your life. By now, you are aware of your patterns of behavior and thought. You have acknowledged that your unconscious mind is in control and recognized your false truth. Now you have to go deeper into the unconscious and remember the details of the actual event. By remembering, you can reexperience the intense emotions and draw a clear link between then and now. Those same emotions are still affecting you and controlling you today. Realizing the events and your reaction to them is the starting point. Regaining access to the felt experience of them is how your awareness becomes insight.

You are in the process of getting to know yourself and your true, secret history.

Like many of my patients, you might be thinking, "I have no idea where my false truth comes from, or even how to begin to figure it out."

You have already begun the excavation. In the previous chapter about unconscious anticipation and expectation, you gathered clues and inched closer and closer to the core of your pathogenic belief. Now you'll continue that journey inward to the precise moment your sense of self took shape. I'll provide specific tasks and guidance as you peel back the layers of memory. How will you know when you arrive at the beginning of your false truth? Look for a sinking feeling, the telltale sign of insight.

Even if you can't recall the exact moment, and you come out of this chapter with only a fuzzy recollection, don't worry. There are many steps yet to go, and how you came to be who you are might become clearer later on. Some therapists skip this part altogether and move directly to behavior modification and intention statements—the "practical stuff." For them, insight and probing of the unconscious mind aren't necessary for change.

Having seen the magic of insight in my office, I believe that knowing the circumstances that led to the development of your false truth and seeing how it has been repeating throughout your life is the key to transformation. With insight into the formation of you, change will be so much more meaningful, lasting, and profound. It's the difference between putting new sheets on a saggy old mattress and getting a brand-new bed.

For a brighter future, you have to see the past clearly. Tracing your past history is all about clarity and reality. As a little kid, you had to deal with your parents because you needed them. You don't depend on them for survival anymore. You can rely on yourself and others. You can leave the damage from childhood in the past where it belongs. But you have to know exactly what the damage is before you can separate from it.

What you're about to do might be a little frightening. It might be frustrating. You might pull back the curtain of memory and see something that surprises or disheartens you. Your mind might have put up protective barriers around the childhood trauma or microtraumas. Your false truth has been in place for a long, long time, and your psyche might not give it up so easily. But by the end of the process, you'll finally have the answer to the question, "Why do I do what I do?" Insight is worth the effort. The joy and relief of understanding beats the confusion and fear of ignorance every time.

If you start out knowing only that you are clueless, great. You're in the majority of people whose childhood false narratives began before age seven, when memories are dim and you couldn't put what was really happening in your home into context. It's amazing what you notice when you look back at your childhood with an adult perspective.

DISCOVERING THE FALSE TRUTH

Daria

The one person Daria always counted on in her chaotic life was her twin. When her sister married a businessman like their "materialistic and superficial" father, Daria felt betrayed.

I pointed out how often she used the word *betrayed* in our discussions.

Nothing is random. Everything is relevant.

"Tell me about your childhood?" I asked her. Often, the first story a patient tells reveals an important enduring issue that influences present-day experience.

Daria told me a story from when she was very small, age four or five, and she was spending rare time with her mother. In general, she told me, her parents were seemingly caught up in her and her sister's busy schedules, which Daria regarded as "silly and superficial." She craved a "real reaction" from them and acted out with intensity and, in her eyes, emotional honesty. Her mother didn't soothe or comfort her; her sister did.

It was obvious to me that Daria's false truth was a reaction to having busy parents who didn't really get her and were unintentionally dismissive. She maladapted by becoming "difficult" in order to get their attention.

Daria prided herself on her "truth telling," but the effect on her relationships with friends and colleagues was nearly always negative. They thought she was too intense or downright obnoxious. When she was rejected, her response was, "They can't handle me."

Daria had recently moved to Los Angeles to work in film and spent much of every session with me talking about how she hated LA because everyone was aloof, busy, and unfriendly. Interestingly, as much as her move to LA made sense given her work interests, it also made sense in reinforcing her worldview that people are caught up in their own lives, are superficial, don't care about anyone but themselves, and don't say what they really feel. In my practice, I see this reaction all the time. We often gravitate to circumstances that reinforce our false truth or prove it right. This played out for Daria in her choice of career in an industry that's all about rejection, in her relationships with noncommittal men, and in her hostility toward her family.

What Daria perceived about being ignored was the cumulative effects of being dismissed as "sensitive" and "difficult" by them. Daria's issues came to a head when her twin, the person who provided the only consistency, comfort, and validation she knew, seemed to abandon her and subsequently take their parents' side after getting married.

Childhood Narrative Clue #1: Identify Intense Emotions

The ultimate shrink question: "How does that make you feel?"

Therapists ask this so often because part of uncovering your childhood narrative formation is connecting behaviors with emotions. A lot of people can't even say how they feel. Putting a name on an emotion is essential for gaining insight.

Try this experiment. Fill in the blanks in the following sentences:

If I skip lunch, I feel _____.

If I don't sleep well, I feel _____.

If I stub my toe, I feel _____.

Easy. You can quickly identify physical sensations like hunger, fatigue, and pain and anticipate accurate outcomes.

It's another story when you try to identify emotions that come up in complex situations and relationships. Although being insulted or abused might make you feel physically sick, I'll ask that for the upcoming section, you disregard physical sensations and focus solely on the emotional.

Fill in the blanks again.

If I break a promise to myself, I feel _____.

If someone ignores me, I feel _____.

If my partner and I have a big fight, I feel _____

_____.

It's hard to pinpoint exactly how you feel in murky emotional waters. For one thing, more than one emotion might come up, which is how humans work. We are capable of feeling many things simultaneously. Often, the immediate emotions you associate with certain situations are the closest to the surface. But if you dig a little bit deeper, you will find an underlying emotion or two that is far more powerful and intense—and revealing—that stems from your false truth.

For insight to be unleashed, you need to put a name on those underlying, *hidden* emotions.

Remember the patient I mentioned earlier with the weight problem who used a clicker to tune in to her inner monologue? I once asked her how she felt after a binging episode.

"Bad," she said.

"Bad in what way?"

"Ashamed, angry, guilty."

We discussed these surface emotions that she associated with overeating—the shame, anger, and guilt. After talking for only a few minutes, she realized that they were all extensions of a single hidden emotion.

"I'm afraid," she said, tearing up. "Afraid that I have no self-control at all and that I'm going to feel ashamed, angry, and guilty for the rest of my life."

This intelligent woman with a strong motivation to change had no conscious idea that she was living in fear, and that fear, more than anything else, defined her. This insight didn't make her stop overeating that very day. But getting to the root of her feelings gave her something to think about besides her kneejerk self-loathing and anger. She came in the following week and said, "Binging causes a lot of anger and self-loathing, but it does *nothing* to make me less afraid for my future. I need something that makes me less afraid, not more ashamed." Shining a light on her hidden emotion turned her thought pattern upside down in one week.

WHEN THOUGHTS CHANGE, BEHAVIOR FOLLOWS.

Many patients ask, "Why is the hidden emotion buried? Why do we have to peel back the layers to discover it?"

To answer that question, let me explain one of the ways pathogenic beliefs solidify. Children often have their genuine "felt experience"—what they actually feel—overridden by a parent's authoritative version of what's going on. If a child says, "I'm scared," and a parent says, "No you're not," the child is being told to disregard the real, genuinely felt emotions in favor of the parent's version of her experience. If the parent's version is incongruent with the child's, then the child is taught and encouraged to reconfigure her beliefs, lie to herself, and deny her true emotions. This disconnect is the main reason it's so hard to understand exactly what you really feel. The disconnect is universal. Even if a parent never said, "You're wrong," a child perceives a change in her mother's facial expression or other instinctive cues that makes her want to suppress her real feelings and change her behavior to please the parent. Readers who are parents will start to notice how they subtly override their children's emotions with an authoritative correction, believing it's "for their own good" or "to toughen them up."

As children grow and develop, they supply their own authoritative voice that consciously or unconsciously instructs them to deny their genuine feelings. It's essential for adults to strip away the dismissive authoritative voice in their heads, to stop telling themselves what they should feel and to tune in to what they actually feel.

Think back: When was the first time your felt experience was challenged and dismissed? If you can identify your dominant hidden emotion, you can trace it back through your childhood to the false truth.

THE SHARP FOCUS: Pinpointing the actual moment or event or series of events that caused the formation of your false truth is a tall order. Most of us have a hard enough time being specific about how we feel at any moment on any given day. The good news is that with a little guidance and thought, anyone who cares enough to try—yes, you too—can learn to isolate and identify your dominant hidden emotions. From there, it's just a few more steps across the bridge to insight. My best advice as you zero in on what set up your false truth is to allow yourself to be confused and uncertain. Allow any feeling that comes up at all. As I've mentioned before, nothing is random. Whatever you feel and whichever memories come bubbling up are *always* relevant to the process. We will make sense of them all.

INSIGHT TOOL:

Name That Negative Emotion

Positive emotions will come into play later on in the book, and they will become dominant in your life very soon. But right now, I'll ask you to explore negative emotions to learn about yourself and your past.

The list of negative emotions below has been organized into three categories of "primary emotions," namely *anger, fear,* and *sadness*—the biggies—and their sub-emotions:

> **Anger:** aggression, annoyance, bitterness, contempt, defensiveness, disgust, disrespect, envy, frustration, hate, hostility, irritation, jealousy, outrage, rage, resentment, revulsion
>
> **Fear:** anxiety, avoidance, caution, concern, doubt, insecurity, intimidation, panic, stress, tension, terror, vulnerability, worry
>
> **Sadness:** apathy, boredom, depression, despair, disappointment, disillusionment, embarrassment, grief, guilt, loneliness, need, regret, rejection, remorse, shame

Do any of these words jump out at you? Do they ping your radar or trigger a strong reaction? Circle them. Strong reactions are clues that'll point you to the relevant events from the past. The stronger the reaction, the bigger the clue.

Read the circled words again, and ask yourself for each one, "Do I have *experience* with this feeling?" Is it familiar? Is it old, going way back, something you've felt for a long, long time? If so, highlight it. Obviously we've all felt many of these emotions from time to time. Highlight only the ones you are *very* familiar with and know extremely well.

Why do this exercise? Reading these words and connecting to what they mean is a way to unlock the unconscious guilt, shame, fear, or resentment that you have suppressed, buried, or denied. It's how you begin to bring the hidden emotions that define you up from the unconscious into the conscious, where you can analyze them.

You might have highlighted a dozen words or only a few. There is no right or wrong number. The objective is to get a working handle on your emotional reactions to increase the breadth of your self-awareness.

DISCOVERING THE FALSE TRUTH

Larry

Like many men, Larry equated his self-worth with his professional success, or in his case, professional stagnation. After earning a master's degree in political science at a prestigious college, Larry got a job as a consultant. He figured out a way to appear affable in the workplace but described himself as "always angry" and insecure. Despite modest success, he felt "like a failure."

Larry married a highly accomplished woman who was far more successful than he was. Although he enjoyed her success—and the power, money, and travel that came with it—he felt overshadowed by her. This "second fiddle" insecurity is what led to his affairs with younger, unaccomplished women. To him, it seemed obvious that he chose his girlfriends as a reaction to his insecurities.

Then we went farther back in time to his childhood. An only child, Larry was raised in rural New Hampshire. His father worked as the general manager of a textile mill and although kind, was inaccessible. Larry's mother was his main caregiver. She was an overbearing, demanding woman who pushed her son to achieve and criticized him when he didn't.

I asked him to describe his emotions from that time. He came up with *angry, disappointed*, and *resentful*. He said, "I was never good enough for my mother, and when my father was around, he tried to calm Mom down by saying, 'It doesn't matter.'" His father didn't care if his son made a mess or got a bad grade, but what the child heard was "Larry doesn't matter." He was torn between believing he couldn't measure up (Mom's authority) and that it didn't matter if he did anyway (Dad's authority). By marrying a successful, driven woman, he confirmed his worst beliefs of himself: he'd never measure up to her and his work didn't really matter anyway. Suddenly his lifelong habit of procrastination and corner cutting made sense.

"Growing up, I was torn between feeling inadequate and feeling insignificant, and that created a deep insecurity and resentment. As a result, I slacked off, actually creating a self-fulfilling prophecy. I felt angry at myself for being such a loser but had to pretend like I didn't care that I didn't matter."

Larry had always believed he cheated on his wife because he felt emasculated. But the affairs were truly his attempt to confirm his belief that his actions were insignificant.

Curiously, this is quite typical of how the mind works. While Larry was unconsciously trying to confirm the notion of his unworthiness, part of him was working to establish that he actually had some game, albeit in a highly maladaptive way. *At the same time*, Larry was both replaying his false truth to confirm it and making an attempt to find another truth and get a glimmer of an alternative, better way to experience himself in a relationship and in the world.

The mind is a marvel. It's always twisting and turning over itself. Insight comes when you iron it all out and it suddenly makes perfect sense.

INSIGHT TOOL:

Visualize Negative Emotions

Another way to discover the hidden emotion in you, the one you have buried deeply, is visualization. How to visualize? Try it by following a step-by-step progression:

1. Begin with acceptance. You have a story to tell. Deep down, you know it very well. It is a story that explains the lion's share of your distress in life.

2. What emotion is very familiar and most troubling to you?

3. If you can't access what this intense emotion might be, imagine that it is in a room behind a closed door. See yourself approaching that door. Open the door. What is inside the room? What shape is it? What color? Does it have a scent? Does it make any noises? Slowly describe the feeling.

4. Double-check that there isn't an even more deeply held, more centrally important emotion lurking in the corner of the room. If you become aware of one, take hold of it and describe it by color, shape, smell, and sound.

5. Back out of the room, leaving the emotions behind, and close the door.

Write down what you saw.

In the room where I hide my dominant emotion, I found

_____

_____ .

The name of this emotion is _____

_____ .

Childhood Narrative Clue #2: Identify Attachment Style

The next exercise in clue gathering uses attachment theory, developed by British psychoanalyst John Bowlby in the mid-20th century. (For more about attachment theory, see page 230.) Bowlby believed that we could diagnose emotional problems by observing how a child behaved in the company of his primary caregiver.

Taking the theory to the next level, psychologist Mary Ainsworth conducted lab experiments by putting a mother and her one-year-old baby in a room together, then having the mother leave the room, and after a short period of time, reuniting her with her baby. The experiment was called the "strange situation."

- A secure baby (60 percent of participants) cried and got upset when the mother left, tried to find her while she was gone, and was comforted by her when she returned.

- An anxious baby (20 percent) became extremely upset when separated from the mother, wasn't comforted when reunited, and seemed not to know how to react—whether to be glad to see her or to be angry at being left.

- An avoidant baby (20 percent) didn't seem to care about being separated from the mother, and when she came back into the room, the child ignored or avoided her by giving his attention to a toy.

Why did different children react differently to the stress of the strange situation? The baby's behavior said more about the quality of the parenting than about the personality of the child. Secure babies' parents were sufficiently responsive, consistent, and attentive. Anxious and avoidant babies' parents were unresponsive, inconsistent, and neglectful to varying degrees.

Bowlby believed that a baby's attachment style stayed the same into adulthood. Researchers in the late 1980s explored the theory that people sought the same parent-child attachment style in their adult *romantic* relationships.[7] In the late 1990s, researchers confirmed that we unconsciously seek out familiar attachments as adults to strengthen our belief that the way our parents raised us is how relationships are supposed to be.[8]

THE SHARP FOCUS: Knowing your adult romantic attachment style can open some closed memory doors about your childhood. Any exercise that helps you look at life from a slightly different perspective will sharpen the focus on how you became you. Here's a helpful quiz to suss out your relationship style.

INSIGHT TOOL:

Attachment Assessment

1. When your partner says, "How do you feel?" it makes you:

    a.   Cringe. I don't like to talk about my feelings.

    b.   Ramble. I love to talk about my feelings, but I don't think my partner is really listening.

    c.   Focus. I ask myself, "How *do* I feel?" and give an honest answer.

2. When your partner is down or in trouble and turns to you for help, it makes you feel:

    a.   Annoyed. I'm not his or her shrink.

    b.   Happy. I'm glad he or she trusts me enough to open up and that my advice is worth something.

    c.   Upset. I worry that my advice or solace won't help, and that he or she will realize I'm not good enough and leave me.

3. When your partner is in an affectionate mood and wants to get close, you feel:

    a.   Delighted. I love being affectionate!

    b.   Uncomfortable. Too much cuddling makes me squirm.

    c.   Relieved. If he or she wants to be close, then he or she isn't going to leave me.

4. You worry about your partner being unfaithful or falling for another person:

    a.   Always.

    b.   Sometimes.

    c.   Never.

5. How would you describe the balance of love in your relationship?

    a.   Equal. We love each other the same.

    b.   I love my partner more.

    c.   My partner loves me more.

6. When something is weighing on you, you usually:

    a.   Confide in my partner first, since he or she is my most trusted friend.

    b.   Confide in my partner eventually. I don't want him or her to judge me harshly. Besides, what's usually weighing on me is something he or she did!

    c.   Keep it to myself. My problems are my business and will only lead to more uncomfortable, probing conversations.

7. Do you keep secrets from your partner?

    a.   Sometimes. I try to be honest, but if I share everything, he or she might get scared and run away.

    b.   Of course!

    c.   Hardly ever, and nothing major.

8. If your partner isn't meeting all of your emotional needs, you feel:

    a.   Good. I'd rather he or she didn't try to "fix" me. I'm fine on my own.

    b.   Angry. I care so much about my partner's needs. The least he or she can do is make an effort to care about mine. If he or she doesn't, it's a personal insult.

    c.   Annoyed. It bugs me if I feel neglected, but I make a point of asking for what I need and being honest about my feelings.

9. When you talk about something that makes you feel insecure, your partner is:

    a.   Reassuring. He or she tries to make me feel better.

    b.   Dismissive. He or she brushes off my concerns and it pisses me off.

    c.   Stunned. I never reveal too much about my insecurities, so if I did say something, my partner would probably be at a loss.

10. The majority of your previous breakups were:

    a.   My call. I didn't see the point in continuing.

    b.   My partner's call. I got clingy and demanding and he or she couldn't take it.

    c.   Mutual decisions. We grew apart.

Scoring

1. a (3), b (2), c (1)

2. a (3), b (1), c (2)

3. a (1), b (3), c (2)

4. a (2), b (1), c (3)

5. a (1), b (2), c (3)

6. a (1), b (2), c (3)

7. a (2), b (3), c (1)

8. a (3), b (2), c (1)

9. a (1), b (2), c (3)

10. a (3), b (2), c (1)

Attachment Style Profiles

Secure (10–15 points): For you, relationships tend to be satisfying, grounding, and supportive. You don't *need* to be in one, but when you are, it's a positive addition to your life and not a source of constant worry or distraction. You tend to be confident in your partner's ability to meet your needs and in your ability to meet his or hers. The partnership is trusting and mutually reliable, but not overly dependent. During hard times, you can count on each other to lift the other up. During easy times, you celebrate the good fortune together. You are each other's biggest fan and sounding board. The connection is reality based, meaning you have a realistic understanding of who your partner is, his or her good qualities *and flaws.* Neither one of you tries to control the other. When you argue, as all couples do, your goal is to resolve the issue or compromise to find a solution. If your partner said, "I'm going away for the weekend with my friends," you'd wish him or her well and then make plans of your own.

Anxious (16–20 points): For you, relationships tend to be sources of stress and worry, and yet when you're single, you feel desperate to find a new partner. You tend to overlook or romanticize a partner's flaws. He or she is like a fantasy figure more than an actual person, which causes problems when he or she fails to meet your unrealistic expectations. Although you long to feel close and intimate, you also fear that expressing your feelings will scare partners away. You believe that you are the one who loves more in the couple and are in constant anxiety about being left for someone better. If your needs aren't met, you become angry and upset and tend to yell or cry. Your partner might respond to the outburst with confusion or frustration, not really sure what happened to set you off. Even if the relationship isn't going well, you cling to it because any relationship is better than none. You are likely to be demanding, possessive, jealous, and insecure, behaviors that might bring about the end of the relationship. When it's over, you say, "I *knew* he/she didn't really love me."

Avoidant (21–30 points): For you, relationships feel like more trouble than they're worth. Although you have a basic human need for companionship, you like to keep your partner at arm's length, and you get very nervous when someone tries to get too close. When a partner attempts to break down your walls, you react by withdrawing or needing "space." You don't rely on your partner for emotional support and would prefer it if he or she were as independent as you are. When a partner asks you to do something, you are likely to blow it off or respond with half measures to prevent future demands. It's not selfishness, per se; it's self-preservation. Besides, you don't ask him or her for support or comfort, so why should you be expected to supply it? At times, the pressure of reciprocity gets to you, and instead of distancing or shutting down with apathy as usual, you explode and storm off. Mutual trust, love, and support seem frightening or strange to you. If a partner gets fed up and leaves the relationship, you shrug, say, "I don't care," and remind yourself that you don't need the aggravation—until the next time you get caught up in a relationship.

According to research, 30 percent of people will undergo a change from their childhood attachment style as adult experiences pile up.[9] Some people might start out as anxious or avoidant and then become secure as an adult by lucking into a nurturing relationship or by doing a lot of work on their emotional health. Some might have had a secure parent-child attachment as a baby or toddler, but become anxious or avoidant due to the development of a pathogenic belief.

FIRST IMPRESSIONS

Carrie

Carrie, a 25-year-old woman who initially came to see me after a bad breakup, took the attachment assessment. She scored as *avoidant*.

When Carrie was five, her father died of cancer. Her mother held the family together and was outwardly strong. When Carrie got upset about missing her father, her mother reassured her by insisting their family would be "fine."

"I remember one night, Mom cracked," Carrie told me. "She started crying on the couch, and said, 'What are we going to do?' For some reason, I grabbed a broom and started to sweep the floor. I said, 'I'll take care of us.'" Seeing her ordinarily strong mother cry was deeply disturbing to Carrie. Picking up that broom—and the burden of strength—became the way she protected herself. She developed the pathogenic belief that she had to ignore her pain and appear strong to survive. Now as a young woman, whenever she feels sad, doubtful, or insecure, Carrie beats herself up about it, compounding the negative emotions with her belief that down deep, she is on the verge of crumbling. By denying her felt experience, Carrie is in constant battle with her true self.

"When I was five, my father died, and I believed that I had to be strong no matter what. When I feel vulnerable in any way, I'm filled with dread that I don't have what it takes to survive in the world," she realized.

The pattern repeats when Carrie is overwhelmed by the smallest obstacle or setback. She's so afraid of showing vulnerability that she cuts and runs from her relationships at the first sign of real intimacy, thereby reinforcing her belief that she'll never make it in life.

It bears mentioning that adults with secure romantic attachment styles are still dealing with hidden emotions and childhood misconceptions. Just because you have an open, mutually reliable, and attentive relationship does not make you immune to suffering in other areas of life or even within your secure relationship.

Your Attachment Style	Common False Truths . . .
Secure	. . . are about personal fears and flaws, such as: "I'm a fraud." "I'm a loser." "I'm superficial." "I'm a liar."
Anxious	. . . are about feeling misunderstood and undeserving, such as: "No one gets me." "No one likes me." "I'm not good enough." "I can't do anything right." "I don't deserve to be happy." "I'm unlovable."
Avoidant	. . . are about feeling vulnerable and insignificant, such as: "I don't dare excel." "If I show weakness, I'll be crushed." "It doesn't matter what I do." "It doesn't matter how I feel." "I can't let myself hope for the best."

Childhood Narrative Clue #3: Identify Actual Circumstances

How and when your pathogenic beliefs took shape is the key to unlocking their grip. It's extremely helpful to have a very good idea about the circumstances you were facing when your misconception of yourself and the world began.

But first, let's take a breath. You have done a lot of work already in order to reckon with what brought you to this very moment. You know you need to understand yourself not only in light of your aspirations—what you want for yourself and your loved ones—you also need to shed light on the suffering you have carried around with you and the misconceptions about the world as a whole that have generalized from some specific circumstances in your past that you lived through but that no longer have to define you. You are in the process of breaking free, after all. So with your courage, my experience and support, and our collective determination to succeed, please take a clear look back in order to trace your false truth's origins.

Did you adjust your behavior in reaction to any of the following circumstances? Can you fill in the details?

Did you ever:

1. Hear your parents fight? About what? Where were you?

2. Feel or fear the loss of a parent by death or divorce? How did your family change due to the loss?

3. Remember being alone in a room, lonely and scared, and no one coming when you called? What were the circumstances?

4. See a parent incapacitated by illness? What happened to the family as a result?

5. See a parent incapacitated by drugs or alcohol? What substance and what pattern of use? How did this affect everyone? What happened to you?

6. Remember being yelled at by an authority figure? Who? What was going on? How did you respond?

7. Listen to criticism from or feel humiliated by a parent or authority figure? What did they say? When did this happen? What did you do when this happened?

8. Feel confused by and wary of a parent's inconsistent behavior? What behavior? How was it inconsistent? How did you understand what was happening?

9. Try to become the person you believed your parents expected you to be? What did they expect? How were you not that person? How did you change?

10. Feel ignored when you expressed your thoughts or needs? What was the opinion, thought, or need? In what circumstances did this occur? What did your parents say or not say? What was the result for you?

11. Feel overshadowed by a sibling? Which sibling? How were you overshadowed? Were words spoken about it? How did you respond?

12. Witness a parent's unraveling? How did he or she unravel? Where did it happen? What were you doing? How did you cope?

13. Endure physical or sexual abuse? Do you remember the time, place, age you were, or any other specifics? How did you make sense of what was happening? To whom could you safely turn? What have you been able to do to gain comfort and support?

14. Remember being mocked or attacked by a parent, authority figure, or peer? Would you consider this verbal abuse? Do you recall any particular words? Was there anything available for you to do to make the situation better? How did you react?

15. Feel like you had become a burden? To whom? In what circumstances particularly? How did you react? By doing what?

INSIGHT TOOL:

Think Backward, One Memory at a Time

Intense negative emotions are clues to how you felt when your false truth began. It's quite difficult for an adult in their 40s or older to recall specific events from childhood. But they can remember something that happened to them last week or last year that gave them the same intense negative emotion. Emotions are in stacks. We store them like that. So start with today and work backward in time, one memory at a time, as far as you can go. Here's the optimal way to do it:

1. Find a calm, quiet place. Sit down in a comfortable chair, and close your eyes.

2. Picture the word for your dominant intense emotion in your head, and conjure up the physical sensations that go along with it.

3. Recall the most recent time you felt this particular way. What happened? Who were you with? What were you doing? What were you thinking?

4. Like jumping from one stone to another in a stream, jump a little farther back in time to another memory of feeling this same way. What were you doing this time? Who were you with? What were you thinking?

5. Keep jumping farther back in time, holding on to the chain of this particular feeling. Go as far back in time as you can.

6. When you start to feel frustrated with your memory, stop the exercise and try to pick up the chain again the next day, ideally at the same time of day and in the same quiet, comfortable place.

7. Link your dominant intense emotion to the earliest memory you can access, even if it's from junior high (where you are certain to have material to draw from).

8. Putting down on paper the intense emotion from childhood that still sets you off in adulthood will help you unlock more memories and understand the link between your current problems and your past. The more familiar you are with the origins of your false truth, the better equipped you will be to get rid of it. Fill in the blanks in the following paragraph:

When I was much younger, I felt very_____
[intense emotion]. My earliest memory of this feeling was age____,
when I experienced_____

_____
_____ [describe
what happened]. To this day, I remember the _____ [intense
emotion]. The emotion is always with me, in a sense. It is triggered
from time to time in my current life, and when that happens, it
deeply affects me. Whether or not anyone knows, would understand,
or would believe that I feel this way down deep, I know that I do. I
carry_____ [intense emotion] around, and it organizes much of
my experience and understanding of how I feel about myself and
what I expect as I go through life.

Once, when I was talking with an adolescent and I asked, "What is your first memory?" she replied, "I don't know. I don't have a first memory." So I asked her, "Well, what is your second memory?" And of course, she had one and told me about it, and we went forward together from there.

It can take multiple sessions of memory jumping to go back as far as you'd like to go. You might never access any memories before age five, which is quite common. But *something* will come up as you push backward. A man I counseled recently had been a heavy marijuana smoker for 30 years and his long-term memory was shot. But he said, "I don't remember anything specific about my childhood home. The color of the house, the furniture, the street. But I remember how my stomach flopped when I got off the school bus at my stop and had to go home every day." Another patient said, "All I remember is feeling like an alien wherever I was. At home, at school. I sat in the corner and watched the other kids like they weren't my species."

Many patients, friends, and colleagues have said to me, "I can't pin down what happened to me as a kid that led to my false truth. Should I ask my parents or siblings about it?" We all have unique reactions to things, and asking someone else about yours might be a waste of time. But if you trust the person, his or her recollections might jog your memory.

Before you turn to others, try "shrinking" yourself. I often ask people questions in casual situations to immediately get a picture of what their lives were like growing up and how they saw themselves in their family structure. "What is your first memory?" and "Tell me about growing up in your family" are two of my all-time favorites. Ask yourself the following questions to expand your knowledge of self. If you record yourself in a voice memo and then play it back, you might be quite surprised by your own answers. Sometimes, you will say out loud the one thing you really need to hear. You don't have to do all of them at once. Start with the first question, and move down the list at your own pace.

> What is your first memory?
> Tell me about growing up in your family.
> What was your life like growing up?
> Were you close with your parents?
> Who was the boss in your family?
> What was your role?
> What did your parents expect of you?
> What didn't they tolerate?
> If you were punished, what did you do in response?
> When people got angry, how did you react?
> What made you feel safe?
> What made you feel scared?

DISCOVERING THE FALSE TRUTH

Bobby

Bobby, 53, a single record-store owner, was in dire straits when he came to see me for the first time. Some of his so-called friends, ones he'd hired to help him with his bookkeeping and management, had swindled him out of a lot of money, and he found himself with huge debts. In therapy, he hoped to figure out how he'd gotten into this mess.

His childhood wasn't easy. Bobby's father, a pharmacist, was an alcoholic. His mother was submissive and co-dependent, and his frat bro–type brothers teased him for being overweight and different. They were into sports and action movies and getting drunk on beer. Bobby was always into music and the arts and never fit in with his family's anti-intellectual preferences. He escaped his rural home life and moved to Boston, where he found an alternative family while hanging out in clubs and in the music scene. He got a job at a record store and eventually became its owner. He finally felt at home there with this somewhat old bunch of vinyl lovers.

"They become the family I never had," he told me. But this new family was full of self-destructive people—drug addicts, the chronically broke and unemployed, and people who always needed a handout. Bobby was there to help. Being a "good friend" had contributed to his current situation.

Bobby thought he'd escaped his family and created a new one in Boston. But I pointed out that he'd really just re-created the same instability of his childhood home of addicts and unreliable people who didn't support *him*.

He had long believed his problem was based on his father and brothers' criticism for his not being just like them. But at the core, his hidden emotion was helplessness. He had no control in his family and he had even less with his new family of friends at the record store.

"I trusted my friends because they were weirdos like me," he said. He thought he'd found like-minded people. But they really were nothing like kind, supportive Bobby. He'd fallen prey to the all-or-nothing thinking that if he shared common interests with someone, then they must also share values. Bobby was so desperate for connection that he took on risky people who ultimately betrayed him.

"I grew up alone and abused, feeling like an alien, criticized and insecure, and believed that since I couldn't find someone like me, I'd never truly be loved and feel safe," he said.

In fact, he'd averted his own critical eye and brought in a new group of destructive people he couldn't rely on. This was a recurring theme in his relationships with women as well. All of his girlfriends turned out to be "crazy."

By now, you can gather at least a broad-strokes idea about what happened in your past, or you can imagine the circumstances of how your false truth came to be. At the very least, you will know what emotion sets you off, your relationship style, and some memories of events that triggered your dominant negative feelings. Using all the clues you've gathered, write down what you suspect triggered the formation of your false truth. Be sure to include how you felt, the emotions of the people around you, and how their emotions affected you.

My false truth most likely started to form when _____

_____

_____

_____

_____.

Gut Check

Common emotions you may experience at this stage include:

Anger. I think of anger as a "cover" emotion, because it covers up everything else. Underneath anger is often sadness, shame, guilt, and resentment. Know that if you feel angry as certain memories come up, there is probably something lurking one level deeper. Explore that.

Excitement. When something does click and you make progress, you're bound to feel excited. That rush is the effect of dopamine, the "feel-good hormone," hitting your brain's reward center. Great! Positive reinforcement will keep you going.

Frustration. You might feel frustrated if you can't come up with any specific memories. Being blocked is not a personal failing or a sign of deficiency. Accept that you are having a hard time. The Zen approach is to know that all things will be clear to you when you are ready to see and understand them. Let the process unfold, and the memories will come.

Impatience. You want answers, and you want them *now!* Insight does not happen on demand. Insight can't be forced. Memories are more likely to come to you when your brain is distracted or you're a little tired or you're in the shower. Let your unconscious do the work for you. If you get stuck searching for memories, stop trying. They'll come in their own good time, when you least expect it.

PART II

REWRITE

YOUR

STORY

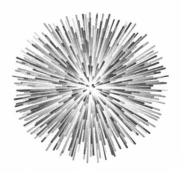

Eradicate the destructive old narrative that has
been a self-fulfilling prophecy for so long,
and construct a new one for the life
you couldn't have imagined before.

REFLECTING ON THE OLD STORY

Since you began this process, you've learned a tremendous amount about who you are and how you became who you see yourself as. You've figured out the false truth that has defined your sense of self since childhood and influenced your relationships, career, and inner basis. Some of these things may still be eluding you. That's okay too; just stay with the process as much as you are able. Insight comes when it comes.

The incorrect, unconscious story you've been telling yourself might be that you're inferior, that you're unworthy, or that you don't deserve love or success. It could be that no one cares about what you do or how hard you try or that you don't matter. It might be the belief that negative emotions are dangerous and should be suppressed, that the weight of the world rests on your shoulders, or that if you aren't perfect, all hell will break loose.

By using the tools I've just shared with you, you were able to recognize your false truth and figure out how it came into existence. You got that sinking feeling in the gut that accompanies insight, the satisfying if unsettling sensation of making a crucial discovery about your life and self. By unlocking this deeply hidden false truth and toggling the insight switch, you have created the possibility for healing and change to begin.

In step one, you learned why change is difficult and that psychological forces are working against you changing your life, but that with courage and faith in the Insight Cure, you can relieve your suffering and experience more joy and happiness.

In step two, I asked you to find patterns of thought and behavior, to appreciate that they exist, and to understand that your unconscious mind is in control of what you say, feel, and do. You used the awareness and insight tools to declare what your false truth is.

In step three, you identified your dominant intense emotion and traced it back in time until you pinpointed the precise circumstances (or as close as you could get) of the formation of your childhood false truth.

Your false truth and takeaway narrative is a major discovery, and you need to spend some time processing and sitting with it. In this chapter, you'll take the necessary step of letting the discovery really sink in. Once again, I'll ask you to go back in time to revisit specific events from the past—from yesterday, last week, last year, or decades ago—and examine how you experienced those events using the new lens on life that insight has provided. If your actions were mystifying to you before, they will make more sense now that you know about the unconscious belief that you always "knew" to be true (but actually wasn't). Insight gives you 20/20 hindsight. You can look at the past and see with crystal clarity how the old story—your expectations of outcomes, your assumptions about life—has been pulling the strings all along.

It takes some time to reflect on how the old story has affected you throughout your life. By dwelling on it, insight solidifies. It goes from being a wispy concept to a rock-solid reality. You can't build your future on an aha moment, no matter how important it is. You have to study that insight, get to know it inside and out, backward and forward. Drag your false truth out of your unconscious and make it as plainly obvious to you as a raisin in a bowl of oatmeal.

To do that, you'll have "go there" and reexperience some painful, disappointing, and embarrassing moments that you'd rather not think about ever again. This can be uncomfortable, but it's the only way to process insight. You will see why relationships have failed and jobs have ended in disappointment, and how your unconscious narrative has plagued you with anxiety and self-destruction.

This step requires you to slow down a bit. I'm not saying you have to analyze *every single event* from your past and register how your false truth undermined your actions and interactions all along. Just shift into a meditative mode and think about things for a few weeks. You might feel impatient to whip through the reflection step and get to the "good stuff" of creating and testing a new narrative. But rushing now would be counterproductive. Before you can move on, you have to look at life events through the new lens and feel excited or dizzy with insight. Patients often tell me, "I can't believe how obvious it all is now!"

After three or four weeks of reflection, you'll find that your excitement is tempered, and you'll feel grounded and sober about what you've come to understand about your life. That's the sign that you're ready to move on.

What to Expect Before You Reflect

In my 20 years as a psychotherapist, I've observed that patients are evenly split in how they anticipate this dwelling step:

They are intimidated by the potential for pain and anxious about their ability to recover from it, or . . .

They are skeptical and dismissive that their false truth from childhood has created a set of largely negative expectations that still defines their lives as adults.

If you are intimidated and want to run from the pain before you even begin: You're right to worry to some extent. Reflecting might be difficult and painful. But fortunately, you will have a wonderful, positive motivation to see you through it: the bright, sparkling new idea that life does not have to be painful, sad, anxious, lonely, or bitter.

You *can* create a new set of expectations that guarantee positive outcomes. Although you came away from childhood with assumptions about life that have held you back, you *can* alter the quality of your inner life and existence. Positive change isn't free. The price might be *some* pain. Because of your past, you might believe that pain and suffering is the whole story and that it's all you'll ever get. It's not. There's so much more on the other side of reflection, a life liberated from old hurts and past pain. Take a deep breath, keep your eyes on the prize, and use a motivational mantra to quiet anxiety.

WHENEVER YOU FEEL A PANG OF ANTICIPATORY DREAD, SAY, "LIFE DOESN'T HAVE TO BE THIS WAY."

When I was a psychiatrist in training, there was a psychotherapist named Leston Havens that I looked up to. He was a local hero, not as well-known outside Boston, but anyone who had training in that area and has been around as long as I have would remember his wisdom and kindness, his incredible way of effecting change in people.

He always said, "First and foremost, we're doctors. Psychotherapy is a medical procedure. And like many medical procedures, it can be uncomfortable. So like any other doctor, you have to provide analgesia—pain relief—and do what you can to help make it less uncomfortable for the patient." In the context of psychotherapy, you make the patient more comfortable by offering warmth, caring, concern, a lively emotional presence, support, and maybe even a little humor when appropriate. All of those important offerings are ways to demonstrate care, and that makes it easier for someone to go through something that they're afraid might be painful.

Being nice is part of the job of a therapist. It's a tool to help people who never would have gotten to insight without love and kindness, or who at least might have taken a lot longer to do it. By reading through *The Insight Cure* slowly and carefully, and by choosing to feel the support that is available through these words and ideas, I firmly believe that you will be able to go through the process and feel amazingly better about yourself and your life. You will feel empowered to the point that no pain you may encounter in this work will prove too great. All you are discovering is the pain you have always known. This book, and this journey, is about relief from this pain.

If you are skeptical: It's quite possible that despite having the awareness that your life could be better than it is, you might still doubt the premise that a minor childhood event is impacting your life negatively to this day. More times than I can count, patients have said to me, "I don't see the connection."

The entire point of the reflection period is to allow your mind to make the connections. Once you know your false truth, just ask yourself, "How has my belief that I'm a loser (or whatever your false truth is) affected my whole life?" Then, even if your conscious mind dismisses the process, your unconscious mind will still give you hints. You'll have a dream about someone you once knew, or a memory will pop into your head. When it does, put that dream or memory under a magnifying glass and imagine how it *could* have been affected by your false truth. Just play along, as if it were a game or puzzle. Ask, "Is it possible this event *is* significant? What might the significance be?" Before long, you'll be playing the reflecting game like a pro and will appreciate its value.

SITTING WITH THE FALSE TRUTH

Steve

Steve's assumption about life was "Every day is great until it comes time to blow your brains out." When he said this to me at an early session, he had a bright smile on his face.

With his characteristic overly cheerful demeanor, Steve described a childhood of extreme stress. His mother, a housewife, was an alcoholic who would go on days-long benders. She would ignore the cleaning and cooking, leaving Steve and his younger sister to scrounge in the kitchen for food. "I learned to cook when I was very young," he said, laughing and showing me a faded burn mark on his forearm. "And I've got the scars to prove it!" He felt an enormous sense of responsibility for his little sister, even though he was incapable of adequately caring for himself. "One time, my sister and I talked to my father and said to him, 'You should divorce Mommy.' We wanted a mother like the other kids, the kind that baked cookies and didn't sleep on the couch all afternoon. But Dad just kept telling us that it wasn't so bad, to just deal with it."

His ADHD undiagnosed, Steve could barely sit still or concentrate on the task at hand or his studies. When he was eight, a few older kids molested him. "They cornered me after school in the playground. It was just that one time, and I didn't see the point in telling anyone about it. It was just a thing that happened. Mom couldn't have handled it. Dad would have been mortified. If I told the teachers, those kids would have kicked the shit out of me. I got over it."

Steve described one incident after another throughout his childhood of things he had to get over. He had survived years of living with extreme stress by sugarcoating it. His false truth was "It'll all be okay," resulting in the unconscious narrative "If I act like it's no big deal and ignore the pain, fear, and sadness, it'll go away." In fact, his life was not okay and ignoring the bad stuff didn't make it go away. His separation, unemployment, and drug addiction were the adult manifestations of his childhood survivalist beliefs.

Steve was skeptical about reflecting on his false truth. "My childhood was fucked up; my adulthood is fucked up. I get it. I don't need to dwell on it."

"Getting it" on a conscious, rational level isn't enough. The purpose of dwelling on it is to connect the intellectual (what you *know*) and the emotional (what you *feel*), and draw an emotional through-line from the past into the present. You have to reexperience emotions to understand them deeply. Steve's tendency to laugh them off was another way he ignored them.

Steve really struggled with taking the process seriously, and we had to work on it for a long time. Skepticism was a thin shield for fear, but until he opened himself up to the process, he wouldn't progress.

How to Dwell Well

To set yourself up for success, follow a few very simple guidelines.

SAME TIME, SAME PLACE

Therapy sessions are scheduled at the same time and same place each week. Have you ever wondered why? There is a reason for this besides simple convenience. The consistency facilitates the process.

Same time. Your unconscious mind learns to anticipate that every Wednesday at 3 P.M., you'll be exploring your emotions. It prepares by floating up bubbles of memory to take into your session with you. So often, patients say things like, "As I was on the subway coming here today, something occurred to me . . ." or "I haven't thought about this story for years, but last night, it popped into my head . . ."

As you begin your reflections on your false truth, it's a great idea to schedule your "self-service sessions" at consistent times. Choose a half-hour period (an hour max) once or twice a week when you can reflect uninterrupted. Like a real doctor's appointment, mark it on your calendar and commit to keeping it. Most medical doctors have built-in incentives for not canceling appointments, charging you the co-pay fee whether you show up or not. However, incentives aren't necessarily productive in the therapeutic context. You can always rationalize your way into or out of things, especially if you are intimidated or skeptical about the process. *Don't cancel on yourself.* If you start making excuses for blowing appointments off, use the mantra "My life can be better" to help keep them.

When can you fit reflection into your schedule?

Circle a day or two.

Monday Tuesday Wednesday Thursday Friday Saturday Sunday

Circle a start time.

6:00 A.M.	6:30 A.M.	7:00 A.M.	7:30 A.M.	8:00 A.M.
8:30 A.M.	9:00 A.M.	9:30 A.M.	10:00 A.M.	10:30 A.M.
11:00 A.M.	11:30 A.M.	12:00 P.M.	12:30 P.M.	1:00 P.M.
1:30 P.M.	2:00 P.M.	2:30 P.M.	3:00 P.M.	3:30 P.M.
4:00 P.M.	4:30 P.M.	5:00 P.M.	5:30 P.M.	6:00 P.M.
6:30 P.M.	7:00 P.M.	7:30 P.M.	8:00 P.M.	8:30 P.M.
9:00 P.M.	9:30 P.M.	10:00 P.M.	10:30 P.M.	11:00 P.M.

Consider yourself committed to that day and that time. You'll learn to associate it with emotional exploration. If your life changes and you absolutely have to change your reflection schedule, go ahead, but try not to bounce around.

Same place. The door of a therapist's office is like a portal between two worlds: the conscious world of decision making and logic and the unconscious world of dreams, emotions, and memories. It's not that you leave "real life" on the other side of the door. It's more like entering a parallel universe where you are of your world but not in it, at least for the next little while.

Most therapists' offices strive for a certain safe and professional tone. Mine was decorated to feel warm and welcoming, with wood-paneled walls, soft-light box lamps, and framed black-and-white abstract prints. It's pleasant but not so distinctive or quirky that the patient would spend more time looking at the furniture than exploring her psyche.

The setting for your reflection should be quiet, distraction free (away from kids, computers, TVs, smartphones), and neutral. If you associate the space with pain and suffering—for example, the bedroom if you're in an unhappy marriage or a home office if you're stressed about work—you might not be able to reflect productively. Ideally, you could find a spot in such places as a park, a library, a quiet coffee shop, or a guest bedroom. A friend of mine once joked that the only way he could find peace when his kids were young was to lock himself in the basement bathroom. If the basement bathroom is your reflecting spot, great. The size and décor of the space don't matter nearly as much as its neutrality and the lack of distractions.

Where will you reflect for your 30-minute "session"?

_____

_____

_____

It might seem like I'm being a stickler about choosing specifics. I wouldn't ask you to commit to the hour and the spot if it weren't an important part of the process. Your mind needs to calibrate to anticipate reflection just as your body calibrates to anticipate meals. You become hungry on a schedule. Your emotional explorations will be more successful if they're on a schedule as well.

Of course, there will be thoughts and feelings, perhaps even some aspects of an insight, that occur at other times and in other places. Just jot them down in a notebook, an e-journal, or a voice memo, and be sure to review and reflect on them at the start of the next regular session.

Reflection Starter Questions

You've selected your time and you are in your chosen spot.

Now what?

Reflection isn't just a skip down memory lane. It's thinking about thinking, thinking about feeling, finding an understanding about how your false truth has colored your life and how you've been living by the old story.

To sort it all out, ask yourself prompting questions and answer them honestly. Then, put each answer under the magnifying glass and refocus (sharply) on how it relates to your false truth. Ask, "How does this event, thought, or memory confirm something I have always believed to be true, but actually isn't?"

REFLECTION QUESTION #1: WHAT WAS IT LIKE GROWING UP IN YOUR FAMILY?

Answer: _____

_____

_____

_____.

When I'm talking with a new patient, I start with a quick evaluation. Does she have a clear sense of her problem today, the one she came to me for help solving? Does she have any awareness or insight about the past? I need a basis of understanding to get started, so we spend a few minutes talking about her upbringing.

To draw a quick biographical sketch, I'll ask, "Where were you born and raised? What was your house like? Who lived in the house? What was your mom like? Your dad? Your brother and sister?" And then I ask the seemingly innocuous follow-up that is actually extremely important: "Tell me about growing up in your family."

The patient pauses. It might strike her as a silly question because she doesn't know where to start. There's just so much material, how could she possibly choose? What story should she come forth with? Finally, the patient will just say *something*, often believing it's random and insignificant.

The amazing thing is, again, the answer is *never* random. It's highly significant, and very likely a direct line to her false truth. Some examples of what people have said include:

> "Typical suburban upper-middle-class life. Except I was the black sheep, never fit in, and was always in trouble."

> "My childhood was fine, but my parents weren't around much."

> "The house was like a busy hive. Lots of people and activity. I was just one of the bees."

I latch on to the grain of false truth in the statement and go from there. "Tell me more about that," I'll say, and we're off. Very quickly, things get interesting.

The big difference between my work with a brand-new patient and you doing your own self-guided reflection is that you already know your false truth. Think of it like a math test. But you have the answer key in front of you, so as you try to solve the problems, you already know where you're going to end up. Reflecting on the false truth is a lot easier than figuring it out in the first place.

SITTING WITH THE FALSE TRUTH

Claudia

I'd initially theorized that Claudia's mother had been neglectful, since hopelessness is a hallmark of having neglectful parents. In fact, she was the opposite. However paradoxically, having super-attuned parents can sometimes have the same effect on a child. No one will ever care as much about Claudia's happiness as her mother, and that has left Claudia feeling disappointed by the rest of humanity. Her isolation has only gotten worse since her mother died.

Claudia's false truth is "I'm going to be let down forever." When her standards for relationships were chronically unmet, when those she chose to spend precious time with inevitably failed to show up in equal measure, she developed the unconscious narrative "I'm going to be the best I can be (as my mother taught me through her example), and people will be inspired to bring their best game too." No wonder she was tired, lonely, and not infrequently hopeless. What relationship could possibly measure up?

As she reflected on the impact of her false truth, Claudia realized the performance high bar she set and her nearly relentless self-sacrifice were impossibilities for casual or close friends, colleagues, or romantic partners to match. Claudia's reflection period was both painful and comforting for her as she reexperienced how her expectations repeatedly soured her reality. It drove some people away and inspired others to take advantage of her, including her "taker" sister, who so easily let Claudia do most all the caring for their mother during her long illness. Through our therapeutic relationship, she experienced the caring and understanding she needed in order to permit relaxing her standard of what she expected of herself and others.

REFLECTION QUESTION #2: WHAT WAS A TYPICAL DAY LIKE FOR YOU WHEN YOU WERE A KID?

Answer: _____

_____

_____

_____.

Painting a very basic picture of a typical day in your house and life can open the doors to insight. This question might be harder to answer because people often don't remember back that far. Don't fixate on specific facts that have to be absolutely true. Just let your mind drift, imagining your daily routine and home life from preschool to third grade.

As you paint this picture of a typical day in the life, ask, "How did I come away from childhood with my false truth?" and "What lesson about life seemed to make perfect sense given the circumstances of my growing up?" In sum, how did the person you envision walking through life from ages four to eight continue on into adulthood? What burdens did you carry then that you still carry today? Confusion? Shame? Self-doubt? A sense that you don't fit in? Feelings of inadequacy? It's not that you're searching only for negative experiences while reflecting. Reflect on positive ones too—times when you felt happy and safe. How does any memory that pops up relate to your false truth?

Focus on the feelings of coming home from school, or having dinner with your family, or interacting with other kids. If you remember feeling vulnerable, lonely, or anxious, connect it to your false truth. Whatever memory comes up from your unconscious will be significant somehow. Use your conscious intellect to figure out how it's relevant to your explorations now.

REFLECTION QUESTION #3: WHAT WAS IT LIKE WHEN YOU LEFT HOME?

Answer: _____

_____

_____

_____.

It might be easier for some people to make connections from more recent history than childhood. So consider and dwell on the emotions of young adulthood. When did you leave home? How did it feel to be on your own? How did you weather the transition? What was it like living away from your family?

You might say, "It was great! I was finally free!" The trouble is you might have gotten away from your family, but most of us bring patterns of thought and behavior along with us even after we become "free." Think about your college or work routine when you stopped living at home. Did any bad habits continue even when you were out of the context of your family?

For example, you might have had physical distance from the critical or neglectful parent, but you were still anxious or self-loathing. Did you continue with destructive behaviors and negative self-talk even away from the circumstances that might have inspired them? Remember my patient with the bad body image and weight problem? When she reflected on her negative self-talk, she realized it was her mother's voice in her head. She carried that with her for decades, hundreds of miles from home.

THE EMOTIONS AND MESSAGES
YOU RETAIN AFTER YOU
LEAVE YOUR FAMILY ALWAYS
RELATE TO YOUR FALSE TRUTH.

Young adulthood is a time when people are making a high volume of new friendships and relationships, some positive and creative, some negative and destructive. Reflect on the people you were drawn to at that age. Did you hang out with a lot of drama queens or emotional vampires? With nurturing, happy people? With users and abusers? With role models and inspirational figures? How did your social circle reinforce your worst—and best—beliefs about yourself? What relationship patterns kept happening again and again when you were newly on your own? To what extent do you see a connection from those patterns to when you were even younger?

The crux of reflecting about this period is imagining yourself as that young adult, walking through life. You have grown and changed, but the burden you carry is the same now as it was then. When you were 20, did you always feel like a fraud, or were you bursting with confidence? Were you chronically embarrassed, excited, hopeful, doubtful, frustrated? It might not seem so important, but if you reflect on dominant themes, you will be able to link them back to your false truth. Always return to these feelings.

One patient, a woman with an absent and disinterested father, had the false truth "I'm unlovable." She created an unconscious narrative of "If I reach out for love, I'll get rejected, so it's safer not to try," and wound up have a string of inappropriate partners, many of them older, that confirmed what she'd always thought to be true. "I always thought I had 'daddy issues,'" she told me. "But now I see that I haven't been looking for a man to make up for the love I missed out on. I've been repeating the cycle of longing and rejection that I grew up with and continue to take comfort in, despite the heartache I feel every time. That is seriously messed up."

The point is, now she knew. Now she had a shot at breaking these patterns and experiencing something more. She cried often as she relived some of her past hurts, but after a month, the sense of loss was replaced with strength. She felt armed to do battle with her demons.

The Sharp Focus: Patients are often confused about what, exactly, they are trying to discover as they reflect. Sometimes I mention the movie *Groundhog Day*. What parts of your emotional life have you repeated over and over again in relationships and other choices, even if they were bad for you? Insightful people recognize the patterns. Your goal during the reflection period is to try to roll with the idea that you are taking a new look at things you've felt in the past, during childhood, adolescence, young adulthood, and adulthood. You are continually replicating the old story. See it, feel it, and know it cold.

SITTING WITH THE FALSE TRUTH

Leo

Leo came to me because of his temper problem. He would fly into rages with friends and family over small things, and then take days to calm down.

In therapy, we figured out that due to his parents' refusal to praise or acknowledge his successes from a very young age (walking, talking) through his adolescence (academic honors) and continuing today (promotions), he developed the false truth "Nothing I do is good enough" and the unconscious narrative "If I work even harder, I might get the acknowledgment I crave." No matter how successful he became or how much acknowledgment he received, it would never feel like enough. His insecurity manifested itself as a vicious temper.

Leo sat with this insight, connecting incidents of rage with feelings of inadequacy from childhood. An overachiever, he devoted himself to the reflection process as if he were starting a new work project.

"I've been looking at times I had temper tantrums as a kid and the adult equivalent later on, especially with boyfriends in college," he said. "Every single rage-out happened right after I felt ignored or overlooked or wasn't given props for doing something I was proud of, even really small things." He described a tantrum he threw when he was a little boy. A friend came over for a play date, and the boy didn't want to play the games Leo had arranged for them. Instead of compromising, Leo got very upset and broke his own toys. "I overreacted in a big way, and I've been doing the same thing my whole life. When I told my father recently about my promotion and he didn't congratulate me, I felt fury welling up inside me. If there had been a Legos track to destroy nearby, I would have demolished it."

For Leo, connecting rage with lack of praise wasn't painful at all. He was excited about toggling the insight switch and impatient to rid himself of the false truth and dispel his anger. I urged him to continue letting insight sink in before the next step, and I made sure to praise his efforts.

INSIGHT TOOL:

Free Association

In your imagining and reflecting, it might seem like you're creating a fiction of your life. Remember that your unconscious mind remembers everything, and what might seem like make-believe has some basis in reality. The thoughts come from somewhere in your head, after all. What pops into your mind might be a blend of memory, movies, books, and family folklore, but the emotions behind the visions are all too real.

To use imagination as a vehicle for insight, try the psychological technique called free association developed by Swiss psychiatrist Carl Jung. A doctor says a word, and the patient then says the first word he thinks of, no matter how irrelevant, absurd, or silly it might seem. The theory is that by taking words out of context and responding without a filter or time for conscious rationalization, your unconscious will reveal itself.

As an experiment, you can try this list of 100 words that Jung himself used to stimulate associations in his patients.[10] Take it for what it's worth. Maybe only five of these words will trigger an intense emotion or unusual response that is worth looking at more closely.

head	mountain	part
green	to die	old
water	salt	flower
to sing	new	to beat
dead	custom	box
long	to pray	wild
ship	money	family
to pay	foolish	to wash
window	pamphlet	cow
friendly	despise	friend
to cook	finger	luck
to ask	expensive	lie
cold	bird	deportment
stem	to fall	narrow
to dance	book	brother
village	unjust	to fear
lake	frog	stork
sick	to part	false
pride	hunger	anxiety
to cook	white	to kiss
ink	child	bride
angry	to take care	pure
needle	lead pencil	door
to swim	sad	to choose
voyage	plum	hay
blue	to marry	contented
lamp	house	ridicule
to sin	dear	to sleep
bread	glass	month
rich	to quarrel	nice
tree	fur	woman
to prick	big	to abuse
pity	carrot	
yellow	to paint	

A more direct and relevant approach to the technique of free association would be scribbling on paper with a pen or typing on a computer, without stopping to fix spelling or grammar, for 10 minutes each day. The point is to just blurt, as it were, onto the page (or screen), without any filters on your thoughts and with no conscious thinking allowed. Don't even look back as you storm ahead. Then take a look at what you've written and try to figure out how it might be relevant to your false truth.

This technique is best done first thing in the morning. You might even keep a notepad next to your bed and use this style of free writing to record whatever you can remember of your dreams. Dreams are like movies from your unconscious that—especially on well-established reflecting days—are trying to tell you something important. Jot down the memory of your dreams quickly, within five minutes of waking, and review your notes during your "session" later.

The Sharp Focus: Free association doesn't have to be forced. It happens all the time, but most of us don't clue into it. If random thoughts come to mind, it's probably a connection to your reflection work. At first, you might not see the connection, but if you refocus, you'll find one. Say you have a reflection session, wrap that up, and then go about your day. Later on, something occurs to you when you least expect it that seems completely off-topic to whatever you're doing—driving, eating, talking in a meeting. It could be a delayed free association of the thinking work you were doing earlier. Keep track of those seemingly new thoughts, which are "new" not in the sense that you've never had them before but in the sense that they are potential clues to deepening understanding and broadening awareness.

Reflection Is Not Storytelling

I was discussing reflection with a friend of mine recently, and she brought up one of the common obstacles people face. "I saw a therapist for a while in my thirties. I remember spending so much time recounting the blow-by-blow of everything that happened in my life," she said. "Conversations with my boyfriends, my bosses, my mother, with tone and inflection. I was so involved in accurately reporting the details that I don't remember making the leap between my current reality and my past beliefs. My therapist just let me go on and on, and would occasionally ask, 'How did that make you *feel?*' We talked about my relationship with my mother a lot but, again, all of it about how we interacted that week. We were completely stuck on current events. I guess having someone to talk to was helpful, but I can't say it was insightful."

As a therapist, I have noticed that some patients seem determined to keep the content of what we discuss in the present tense. They can get very detailed in their stories. We wind up triaging current problems and hit a wall of resistance when we delve into the deeper realms of experiencing emotions and making false-truth connections between past and present that will actually unlock the beliefs behind bad patterns.

Therapy or self-guided reflection is not a daily update. It's about understanding and experiencing how your old story has been the recurring theme of your life. When patients obsess about the minutia of their day-to-day existence, I warn them that reflection is about the big picture, a broad understanding of how your current behavior patterns are an inadvertent replay of your false-truth script from the past.

As you practice reflection, you will settle into letting go of the present and delving into the past. A good sign of success is that you start to do this automatically, which should occur after two or three weeks of self-service sessions.

When I was in residency training at UCSF, there was a venerable CN5 (clinical nurse five, the rank equivalent to a five-star general) named Barbara Tescher. Over her decades of working with patients, she heard thousands of "he said, she said" rehashes between families and couples. She would just shake her head and say, "It's the same old bus coming around again, no matter what's color it's painted." If you don't have insight into the false truth that manifests into patterns, that bus will keep coming around the bend, carrying all those familiar feelings, and you'll get on board every time. But if you recognize the bus for what it is, you'll have the control to say, "Not this time," and wisely let it pass.

INSIGHT TOOL:

The Experiencing Scale

Psychiatrists track their patients' initial capacity for self-awareness, understanding, and insight, as well as their therapeutic progress, by using the Experiencing Scale.[11] The scale measures the seven levels of involvement (listed below) of a patient's connection with events and feelings. Are you understanding events profoundly or merely skimming the surface? Insight is a deep plunge. As you reflect on past events, keep probing your mind, heart, and gut until you reach level six (you'll tackle level seven in the next chapter). In order to get your self-knowledge operational on a deep emotional level, you must develop your capacity to go down this ladder.

1. **You can talk about events and ideas.** For example, "My boyfriend had sex with another woman."

2. **You can talk about yourself without expressing emotions.** "My boyfriend betrayed me."

3. **You can express emotions, but only about external things.** "I was angry and upset when I found another woman's bra in my bed."

4. **You can focus directly on your emotions and sense of self.** "My anger is really a mask for insecurity and inadequacy."

5. **You can explore and express your inner experience.** "Because of my childhood 'I'm unlovable' false truth, I might have purposely chosen a man who would hurt me."

6. **You "get" why you've reacted in certain ways about things you previously didn't understand.** "I see now that my mother's relentless criticism is why I feel unlovable."

7. **You use your new perspectives to understand problems as they occur.** "My childhood of being cut down might be why I'm drawn to cruel people, but I can learn to recognize the pattern and avoid men who I know will be mean to me."

The steps are the ladder. As you go from rung to rung, you get a deeper and greater understanding of yourself, your false truth, and what you expect in the world. As you progress from superficial understanding to deeper insight and reformulation of your experiences, you gain the power to transform and make change.

If you stay on the first few superficial rungs of this ladder, you'll probably feel frustrated because you understand something about what the problem has been, but you really are not empowered to change. In therapy, people often get some understanding of what is making them miserable, but they're still miserable. Then they quit therapy or inner work because they don't think it's actually working. But it would work if they took it down to a deeper level of their heart, where they have the power and the ability to really effect change. You can do this by allowing it to happen, by sticking with the steps and believing that they're working on you whether you realize it consciously or not.

SITTING WITH THE FALSE TRUTH

Carrie

Carrie came to see me after a bad breakup. In our first session, we discussed the impact of her father's death from cancer when she was five and the false truth "I have to be strong" for her widowed mother's sake. It developed into the unconscious narrative that if she showed any sign of weakness, it meant she wasn't capable of handling life. Her terror of appearing vulnerable has made her avoid or sabotage challenging situations like starting a new job or opening up in an intimate relationship.

Carrie was paralyzed by the idea of connecting her childhood anxiety with her adult inertia. "I can't do it," she told me. "It's too hard to think about this stuff." At some point during the reflective period, she was in a bad car accident. If she hadn't been wearing her seat belt, Carrie might have died, but she only broke a rib and sprained her ankle. Incapacitated, she became the two things she feared most: weak and needy.

She called me and complained that she had no food in the house. I suggested she reach out to her friends. "I haven't told anyone," she said. "If I put it on Facebook or make calls and people don't offer to help me, then I'll feel even worse." After some urging, Carrie called her neighbor, who went food shopping for her and kept her company until her family came to care for her while her ankle and rib healed.

The incident made Carrie see all too clearly that her fear of appearing weak made her weak (hungry and miserable) and that asking for help made her literally stronger. It forced her to acknowledge the life-threatening effects of her false truth. Her convalescence was productive in so many ways. Carrie was ready to go deeper into her past and make the necessary connections. "The car accident was good for something," she said. "It made me see things more clearly, and since I couldn't walk, I had a lot of time to sit around and think about it."

Self-Care

In therapy, there are usually two people in the room: the patient and the doctor. While you are reflecting, there will be only one: you.

Eventually, you'll share your journey with a trusted friend or partner, but right now it's important that you figure out as much as possible on your own. You can probably guess the reason for this: The people in your life might be contributing to the manifestation of your old story. The purpose of reflecting is to tune in to the script you've been enacting for a long time and see how it has been repeating. The first person you want to talk to about this might be a main actor in your script. They could be resistant or dismissive about your insights, especially if you realize you have to change your script and their role. In upcoming chapters, I'll give very clear guidelines about how to discuss all your personal revelations with your intimates. Until then, walk this path by yourself (with me as your guide) and give yourself all the emotional support you can.

Forgive Yourself

During the dwelling stage, as it really sinks in that your false truth has been controlling you, you might feel more responsible for the problems in your life. Guilt and regret are often the by-products of successful reflection. You could feel like you've wasted years of your life on a lie or that it's too late to fix things. Seeing the life-long impact of your false truth might cause a meta-reaction, like "I've been such a loser all this time for believing I've been such a loser all this time!"

There is some reality to the fact that as you get healthier, you might regret lost years. It's never too late to change your experience of living and the quality of your interactions with those lucky enough to get to know you. We can't do anything about the past except understand it and forgive. We *can* do a lot about the future if we proclaim that it's never too late to get on a happier track.

I have a 69-year-old patient who first came to see me when he was 59, after his drinking got out of control. He was hospitalized and detoxed a number of times, but he never wanted to go to Alcoholics Anonymous. Finally, he was referred to me, and I've helped him maintain his sobriety for the last 10 years.

We realized he was drinking to self-medicate a tremendous amount of anxiety. The anxiety came from feelings of inadequacy about not making a lot of money or being a captain of industry (as he was expected to be by his parents), and his false truth was "I've got nothing to offer and I let people down."

But he had so much to give to others. He'd been married since age 22 to the same wonderful woman. They didn't have any children, but his nieces and nephews loved him. He had volunteered at a homeless shelter twice a week for years and years. When he comes into the office, I enjoy his presence. Everyone does. He didn't understand or believe any of the positive contributions he'd made to his family, friends, or complete strangers. He just thought of himself as an underachieving loser with compounded shame for almost drinking himself to death.

We worked in therapy to maintain his sobriety and for him to understand that his false truth was not valid. For most of his life, he saw only how he let himself down, and he didn't see others' parallel experiences of him. But now he sees that he's appreciated, and he is quite content in his daily routine. He can touch people's lives and makes a difference that justifies, in his words, "my being on the planet."

At our last session, he said, "I'm so upset with myself."

I said, "Oh no, are you having a temporary emotional relapse? We've been through this for so long. You don't need to let yourself fall prey to those old feelings about yourself. They are so outdated now and they were wrong in the first place, right?"

"No, Doc, that's not it. I've got all that."

"So what is it?" I asked.

"It's just that I didn't get sober until I was sixty. Now I'm pushing seventy. How come I couldn't have met you in my thirties?"

We talked about the fact that, yes, he wasted some years in an anxious, inebriated fog. But he's here now. Life is continuing, and he is dedicated to being better from this point on.

The Sharp Focus: Every single one of us has things to work through. We all have problems to overcome. Past hardships give you seasoning and perspective about what's really important to you. The past is the past. It doesn't matter why it took you until now to conquer your misconceptions from childhood. Perhaps you lacked the maturity or emotional bandwidth to make sense of it until today. Don't regret not having done it before. Be glad you are doing it here and now.

LOVE YOURSELF

Whatever you did or believed, whatever false truth you carried out of childhood, it happened for a reason. You created the old story because you needed it at the time to survive otherwise unmanageable pain and confusion. You were just a kid. As an adult, you can forgive yourself for having misconceptions as a child. You can find a new, successful way to love, work, contribute, and feel fulfilled without that old narrative. You have to trust in the process and make that leap of faith that there is more out there than your experience of life has taught you so far. You've already been working on control mastery on some level, testing out a different way, hoping the world can react to you in better way. Believe that a different story exists for you. Let yourself get excited that change is possible and real.

Love and understanding can help you feel better and move forward. Whether you're refocusing your magnifying glass on the past, the present, or the future, don't think harshly of yourself. Appreciate that whatever happened made sense at the time. It was what you needed to do. Something that you didn't even know was controlling your behavior. You made mistakes, were self-destructive, and didn't know why.

Growing up, your circumstances were not ideal. You were just trying to survive in the world you were born into. But you aren't imprisoned there now. You can make your world. You weren't evil or a fool for your past sins. You can't erase the past, but you can use insight to make sense of it and to be better in the future.

LOVE YOURSELF FOR WORKING HARD TO BE THE PERSON YOU WISH TO BECOME.

Show yourself kindness and compassion, especially when you're looking at the person you used to be. When you're dealing with serious stuff, a positive feeling that says "I'm special" along the way makes the difficult things bearable, even enjoyable.

Along with reading these words of encouragement, you can be your own support system. Be your own cheerleader. Give yourself the kindness, warmth, and humor that a doctor would offer.

INSIGHT TOOL:

TLC

How can you treat yourself with tender loving care during the reflective period? Ralph Waldo Emerson said, "The question and the answer are one," so consider what comfort means for you, and get a lot of it, whether it's great food, exercise, sex, nights out with friends, or time in the garden. Here are some suggestions for boosting your TLC:

1. Get seven hours of sleep per night minimum.
    According to a recent study by researchers at the
    University of California, Berkeley, if you get a full

night's rest, your emotional reactions will be less intense than if you are sleep deprived.[12] What's more, REM sleep, the stage when you dream, soothingly slows the brain's electrical activity. As Michael Breus, Ph.D., a sleep expert, told me, "Science has proven that emotional reactivity is exacerbated by sleep deprivation. During emotional upheaval"—such as reflecting on your false truth for a few weeks—"you really need to get sufficient rest."

2. Try a mind-clearing breathing meditation for a few minutes every day. I practice what is called *square breathing*. (See the instructions for this practice on page 219.)

3. Listen to your favorite music, a few songs to center you and make you feel happy.

4. Spend time in nature, under the sky or by water.

5. Play with a friendly pet.

6. Take a long, hot shower or bath and gently stretch.

7. Do a few yoga poses and hold them a little longer than usual while concentrating on your breath.

8. Make some herbal tea and enjoy.

9. Remember times when you connected with someone with whom you felt close; reminisce a bit.

10. Believe that this process will work and think positively for a few minutes two or three times a day.

As I mentioned earlier, step four takes a while to complete. Over these three or four weeks of reflection, you have made weekly or biweekly appointments with yourself to explore how your false truth has been a recurring thread throughout your life. During those sessions, you used a handful of techniques, including asking yourself questions, morning writing, and free association to jostle loose relevant memories. You've come to appreciate how stubbornly present your false truth has been. Whenever you had a hard time, there it was. Whenever you made a mistake or did something regretful, the false truth was lurking. The Experiencing Scale has shown that on the ladder of insight, the deeper you go, the more you benefit. And lastly, you've initiated the all-important practice of self-care and self-love. You are your own best friend as you learn more about who you are. Loving yourself is how you get better.

Gut Check

As you reflect, you might feel:

Blame and shame. These two often go together at this stage of the process. You feel ashamed of past behavior and blame yourself for it. You were doing what you needed to do, what your set of assumptions caused you do to. You are responsible for your actions, but you were also being controlled by a false truth you were not aware of that was instilled in you before you could have defended against it. What matters now is that you are working to change.

Determination. When you feel centered, like you know your false truth cold, you are ready to move on to the next step.

Excitement. It all makes sense now! The light of insight is shining brightly, and it can fill you with exuberance to see how your past and present are connected.

Frustrated. Reflection requires you to think about and reexperience difficult emotions and events. It's only natural that people sometimes feel frustrated, as if the process is making them worse, not better. What I tell patients is that if you feel worse, you are getting better. It's a sign that you are doing the work that needs to be done. You've avoided these memories and feelings for long enough, and now they have to be brought to the surface to heal. This phase is temporary—a few weeks. Ride it out and know that for the next little while, feeling bad means you're doing well.

WORKING THROUGH THE OLD STORY

Just as there is so much more going on your mind than you were previously aware of, there's so much more of life yet for you to experience. A whole world of possibilities you haven't imagined exists, and it is waiting for you. To start your new life, you have to separate from the old story, put the assumptions of the past into perspective, and change your mind-set once and for all as you move forward with a new story.

Everything I've asked of you so far has been about looking inward to access your past and your unconscious mind. Now I'll ask you to shift the focus outward, into the present. You will start to make concrete changes in your day-to-day conscious thoughts that will alter how you experience life and interact with others.

To turn insight into change, you have to process, aka "work through," what you've learned. Working through is an important concept in psychotherapy, made up of two phases. Phase one is *recognizing resistances*, or seeing your childhood false truth for what it is and understanding exactly how it has impacted your life and become a self-fulfilling prophecy. In other words, flipping the insight switch.

You have been engaged in flipping the switch for the last four steps, and if you have worked well, you are recognizing past resistances as a matter of course. You know what your false truth is, have traced it back to its origin, and have spent weeks reflecting on it. And as a result, you have gained insight into what held you back then and holds you back currently.

Congratulations are in order for all the hard work you've already done! The switch has been flipped, and the light of insight shines from within. Now you can progress to phase two of working through by *overcoming resistances*, or using your recently acquired knowledge to steer yourself in a new direction. During this phase, you will pour the foundation of a new life by shifting your perspective and continually reminding yourself of your intention to shine the light of insight on your thoughts and actions. To overcome resistances and move forward in life, be mindful and present about your moment-to-moment experience. Focus sharply on why you do what you do and feel what you feel.

For a long time in my psychiatric training, I couldn't grasp the concept of working through. Dr. Amini, the man who first challenged us to explain what insight felt like ("a sinking feeling"), told me during my training that insight doesn't automatically create change. Discovering your false truth is such a momentous achievement, and I thought that alone would set someone's life on a different course. But as Dr. Amini kept telling me, "You have to work the insight through." It's not enough just to reflect on the old story, as you did in the previous chapter. You have to keep the insight spotlight switched on bright and aimed exactly where it will illuminate the dark and mysterious corners of your psyche.

The reason I struggled to appreciate working through as a psychiatry resident in training may have been my upbringing as a child. My mom was a resourceful, determined woman. If she wanted something to happen, she supposed that her wish or intent was enough to accomplish her desired result. Results occurred instantaneously in some cases and never in others. To me as a kid, it seemed like her ideas magically turned into reality. Or sometimes, they caused her to get really irritable and retreat to the bathroom. Either way, I didn't witness the grinding process of deliberately working from point A to B to C to G, all the way to Z. I had to learn in my own life, in my own struggles as an adult (and through the teachings of Dr. Amini), that change isn't a matter of merely picking up the phone or enlisting a helpful friend. It's a process of sweating out the details, step-by-step, by yourself.

Your unconscious plays its part in working through by allowing seemingly random thoughts and memories to pop into your head. As you try to understand exactly why you felt/said/did something, look closely at those pops! They are *always* relevant. So are your dreams and daydreams, both products of your unconscious. Have you ever tried to figure out a problem or come up with an idea and just couldn't do it, no matter how hard you tried? In frustration, you might have put it aside and then, after a nap, shower, or good night's sleep, you reexamined the problem and cracked it easily. You can thank your unconscious for solving the problem for you. Part of working through insight will happen while you're in a dreaming, meditative, or semi-hypnotic state (zoning out while you watch TV, staring at the ocean). Help your unconscious do its job by getting plenty of sleep and by meditating for a few minutes each day.

Your conscious mind will do the bulk of the work of working through. It's an intellectual process, after all. It can seem frustrating at times. I think of it like being in a redwood forest that is so dense you can't see a path out of it. You might be trapped there if you didn't have one invaluable tool: insight. The knowledge of your false truth, the understanding that your expectations have been a self-fulfilling prophecy, and the faith that your old story doesn't have to define you and your relationship with the world will light your way out of the forest.

Will light your way, I said. You're not quite out of the woods just yet. You have to keep the light on, keep shining the insight spotlight at every dark shadow. As you pick your way through the forest, cast the beam in every direction, at every situation, relationship, and reaction. Shine it at emotions and experiences that seem familiar to shed light on what's really going on, and then turn that light toward a new path forward. (Remember, if an experience feels familiar, it means you've been down that rocky road before and are repeating old paths and patterns.) Aim it high, aim it low, and before long, the whole forest will be illuminated. The trapped, afraid feeling will be replaced with freedom and hope about what lies beyond the tree line.

To paraphrase a lyric from "Anthem" by Leonard Cohen, everything has a crack in it, which is how the light gets in. In working through, the light is insight. It shines from within. The crack is your understanding of the false truth that once made you feel trapped—and that understanding is how the light gets *out* to shine a way forward.

As a doctor, I can tell you unequivocally that the light in you has *got* to come out.

I'm a believer in meditating on (longish) mantras, and a good one for working through is this: "A long time ago, I wrote a story about myself in relation to the world and took comfort in feeling right about it. The story has been repeating itself in various forms ever since. It's time for that story to end and a new one to begin. I trust that the Insight Cure can get me unstuck from my old story as I work through my new knowledge and understanding."

It's hard, but it's not harder than that.

Unlike recognizing resistances—the exciting *eureka!* of unlocking the secrets of your psyche—overcoming resistances is the "rolling up your sleeves" part of the Insight Cure. It's the gritty, gutsy, glorious sweating in the details, using red-hot insight to melt the residue of the past and get yourself unstuck in the present. You will now begin phase two of working through—turning insight into change—by separating from your old story completely.

It's a lot to take in. I won't pretend it's not. What you're about to do is no trifle. It's an involved journey, and it takes a while—from several weeks to several months—to adequately work through your old story and emerge from the forest into unknown territory. Make a commitment to yourself to make time every week to examine how the old story affects your life by sticking with your regularly scheduled "appointment." Use the time to reflect even more substantially than during the previous step and to increasingly shift your focus away from the past to your present existence.

The work you do now will pay off lavishly. A deep commitment to the process will make the light shine even brighter. You'll have an easier time dealing with crises—minor and major—as they come up in your day-to-day life. Insight is the key that will unlock your potential. Your life will go from feeling ordinary to being extraordinary.

You Are the Hero of Your Own Life

What do Greek mythology's Perseus and Jason have in common with Luke Skywalker, Wagner's Siegfried, Samwise Gamgee from *The Lord of the Rings*, Jesus, and the Buddha? A lot, actually. Their stories unfold with striking similarity. American author and professor Joseph Campbell charted the myths and legends of heroes across cultures and religions in his seminal 1949 book *The Hero with a Thousand Faces*. He organized the classic "hero's journey" into 12 stages, which I have very succinctly outlined here:

1. **The ordinary world.** The hero is introduced; he has an ordinary life and some internal or external conflict gnawing at him.

2. **The call to adventure.** The hero learns that he has to leave his ordinary life and strike out on his own for righteous purposes.

3. **Refusal of the call.** Something holds him back, either fear of the unfamiliar or a person who doesn't want him to face the danger ahead.

4. **Meeting a mentor.** The hero eventually sets out and immediately meets a mysterious stranger who

gives him advice, training, and weapons for the road ahead.

5. **Crossing the threshold.** After traveling out of the ordinary world and into an unknown (often magical) realm, the hero has to learn a new way of life.

6. **Tests, friends, and enemies.** In the extraordinary world, the hero faces monsters and solves puzzles. He picks up allies and adversaries along the way.

7. **Approach.** The hero and his team move ever closer to a major test (more monsters and puzzles) in the extraordinary world.

8. **Ordeal.** During the major test, the hero faces his deepest fears, usually suffering a loss or death, which teaches him important lessons about life.

9. **Reward.** Having survived the ordeal, the hero is rewarded with a gift or treasure, called a "boon." He feels a new anxiety about possibly losing it.

10. **The road back.** With his remaining friends or alone, the hero sets out to return to the ordinary world (home) with his treasure. His enemies are in hot pursuit.

11. **Resurrection.** Close to home, the hero fights his enemies again, usually losing another friend, but emerges victorious and resolves all conflict.

12. **Return.** The hero arrives back home with the treasure and uses it to transform the whole world.

The Hero's Journey

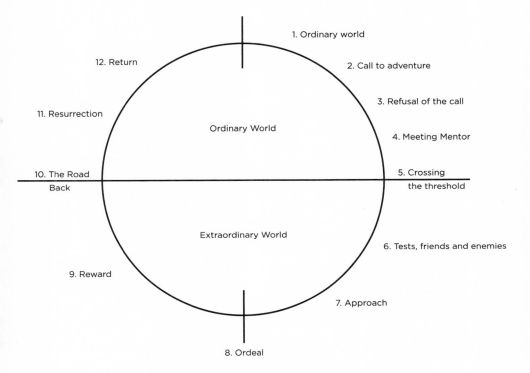

The Insight Cure is wonderfully aligned with the hero's journey. You are the hero of your own life, and you are on a quest. When you began your journey inward, you didn't know who you really were. As you march into unknown worlds (working through) with the help of mentors (or just a humble author), you have to slay your dragons (false truth, old story), and take the boon (new knowledge and deep understanding) home with you for the betterment of yourself, your family, your tribe, and the entire world. One of Campbell's famous lines in *The Hero with a Thousand Faces* is "Where we had thought to find an abomination, we shall find a god; where we had thought to slay another, we shall slay ourselves; where we had thought to travel outward, we shall come to the center of our own existence; where we had thought to be alone, we shall be with all the world."[13]

Another interpretation of the hero's journey that's even more relevant to the Insight Cure was created by Hollywood story development executive Christopher Vogler. He expounded on Joseph Campbell's work in his own best-selling book for screenwriters, *The Writer's Journey: Mythic Structure for Writers*. Vogler's hero's inner journey, about the main character's emotional odyssey, has 12 stages as well. These are identified below, along with my comments on how this emotional odyssey is aligned with the process you're currently engaged with:

1. **Limited awareness of a problem.** You don't have a clue about your false truth (or even that there is one), but you know you're unhappy.

2. **Increased awareness of the need to change.** Things just keep getting worse as you spiral downward in bad habits and behaviors.

3. **Resistance to change.** However painful your life is, you take comfort in the familiar and fear exploring the unknown.

4. **Overcoming fear.** You delve into the unconscious and discover your false truth, shedding the light of insight on your behavior and mitigating the fear of the unknown.

5. **Committing to change.** You make and keep appointments with yourself to face your past and overcome resistances to get unstuck from it.

6. **Experimenting with new conditions.** After working through your old story, you create a new one and test it to reinforce its validity.

7. **Preparing for major change.** Tests start small and get more challenging as you gain confidence in who you have become.

8. **Big change.** You see yourself in a different way.

9. **Accepting the new story.** You believe that the new you is the real you.

10. **New challenges to the new story.** Something happens in life that challenges your new sense of self, but you use the tools of insight to stay on track.

11. **Last-minute dangers.** Life is unpredictable. New challenges and tests always come up, but they don't knock you off your new track.

12. **Mastery.** Your new narrative and sense of self are your much-improved default settings. You have become a new person.

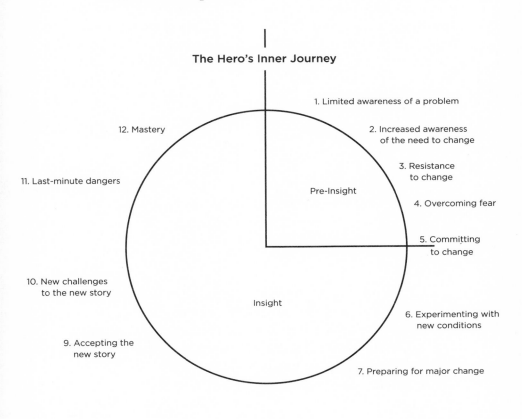

The Hero's Inner Journey

1. Limited awareness of a problem

2. Increased awareness of the need to change

3. Resistance to change

Pre-Insight

4. Overcoming fear

5. Committing to change

12. Mastery

11. Last-minute dangers

10. New challenges to the new story

Insight

9. Accepting the new story

6. Experimenting with new conditions

7. Preparing for major change

8. Big change

The Sharp Focus: Take a look at the illustration of the hero's inner journey. Notice the difference between the insight space versus the pre-insight space. I've mentioned before how much more there is to an insightful life, and this illustrates the concept perfectly. Your world will expand in ways you can't imagine, and you'll go places you never knew existed. You are currently in Vogler's fifth step, *committing to change*, right on the cusp of making major changes. Before you can inhabit your new self, you have to fully overcome resistances created in the past. You are transitioning right now, shedding the last vestiges of your time in emotional darkness. Whenever you have doubts that you are making real progress, know that the only way toward a healthy and happy existence, and relief from suffering, is forward. In fact, there's no going back. Once the light of insight has been switched on, it can't be turned off.

Three Elements of Change

In order to overcome resistances that lead to real, lasting change in your behavior and sense of self, you need a new set of emotional skills—like Greek hero Perseus's shield, sword, and helmet—to take with you on your journey as you progress.

1. DETACHMENT

One catchphrase of psychotherapy that we need to repeat to ourselves often is "The person is not the problem. The problem is the problem." You grew up with a false truth, aka "the problem," a story you told yourself about yourself that has shaped you. But that false truth is not you, "the person."

Externalize the problem by putting it in perspective. Appreciate that your depression, anxiety, low self-esteem, or addiction is not all of who you are or who you have to be. You don't have to react the same way when certain feelings come up. The thoughts and behaviors of the past are *not* all that's available to you.

YOU ARE NOT HOW YOU FEEL. DOMINANT EMOTIONS MIGHT HAVE CONTROLLED YOU IN THE PAST, BUT THEY DON'T HAVE TO ANYMORE.

Say you are at work, overwhelmed and under pressure that is triggering paralysis or rage or sadness. Imagine taking a giant step outside your body and watching yourself react to the stress. Tell yourself, "I don't have to react that way. I don't have to feel _____ _____ [fill in the the emotion you're experiencing]." Imagine that the emotion is a separate entity that can be removed from your body and mind. See yourself standing beside it, and resume your moment-to-moment life without that emotion inside you, controlling you.

When I'm in line for coffee, running late to the office, and someone ahead of me is taking forever, I start to feel impatient and annoyed. I can feel my blood pressure rising and the desire to direct my anger at the person ahead of me. But then I detach from the emotion, look at my annoyance and anger from a distance, and say, "I don't have to feel that." And I do something constructive instead, like review the day ahead or take care of some e-mails.

Another useful metaphor for detachment is what psychotherapists call *conscious objectification of self.* During previous reflection times, I asked you to relive experiences and events from the past. Now, instead of being an active participant in those memories, think of yourself as a dispassionate observer of the scene. You are no longer *I* or *me.* You are *he* or *she.* It's not *my mom* but *a mother.* Focus on the scene with a third-person perspective.

A scene plays a lot differently when you're behind the camera or in the audience than when you're on stage. For one thing, you are not seeing others through the limited perspective of your own eyes and heart. You can watch everyone, including yourself, and gain a new appreciation of all the players' motivations and reactions. Adopting a third-person point of view (POV) makes it easier to move through your day and gives you another layer of understanding about what's going on.

Turn that lens on the past to see how your parents behaved, and perhaps for the first time you will really understand their actions, not just how they affected you. In the Buddhist tradition, detaching from drama or conflict is called *taking the middle path.* You don't take sides. It's not you versus your parents or your circumstances. You are neutral in your observations. Only with this objective detachment can you really let the pain go.

When I detached from my old story, I was able to appreciate that my mother was dealing with her own overwhelming emotions, and my father had trouble being around that. I understand why he had to step back from her and, by extension, me. He was trying to rebuild his life and didn't know how to be a better father. On an unconscious level, I was trying to minimize their suffering by not adding to it with my own. By seeing this clearly with the third-person POV, I could appreciate that my parents were doing the best they could in a hard situation—as was I.

2. ACCEPTANCE

One patient of mine had a particularly painful false truth to work through: When she was a little girl, her father sexually abused her. She survived the abuse by believing she was protecting her beloved mother from the same mistreatment. While detaching from her old story and looking at her life from a third-person POV, she realized that her mother, the woman she worshipped, must have known what was really going on. My patient thought she was saving her mother, but in truth, her mother should have been saving her.

Insight can be shattering. Your construct of what used to make sense is demolished, which can be disconcerting to say the least. My patient's construct that her mother was a saint was destroyed. How do you pick up the pieces of a shattered life construct?

The truth is, you don't. You leave those pieces on the floor and accept that your old story is broken beyond repair. You don't have to twist yourself into knots to keep it whole. Your life is not what it seemed. Stop clinging to lies and fighting reality. Instead, accept the truth and enter the new, unknown world.

Some patients don't want to accept the real truth and would rather put their blinders back on. I remember a different patient, who was an alcoholic, once saying, "I want to go back to blissful ignorance! Those were good days, when I didn't know anything."

I said, "Like when you woke up in the gutter, and then went home to your wife to tell her you got fired again?"

"Well, not that part."

Once you've seen reality for the first time, blissful ignorance might seem attractive, but there's no going back now. If you accept that life is not what you thought it was, you'll overcome resistance to change much faster.

When my patient accepted that she'd mythologized the one sacred relationship of her life, she grieved for herself and felt a lot of anger toward her mother. And then she used the third-person POV to see her childhood through her mother's eyes. "She was a victim of my father too," she said. "Mom was doing the best she could to survive, and looking the other way when he abused me was all she could come up with. It's pitiable and disgusting, but it's what I have to accept about her."

Frailty is the human condition. It is the most important thing to accept about anyone who has failed you, or even about yourself, with your own failings. Being able to work through this understanding of human behavior in all its pitiable complexity requires you to see people in a variety of different ways concurrently. Think of human emotion as a gemstone, with each facet representing a feeling. It's easy to see one or two twinkling sides at first glance. How about three? Or four? Or eight? At the same time?

A multifaceted POV is the difference between a man saying, "I either love my wife *or* I'm really angry with her" and "I can love my wife *and* be really angry with her at the same time."

My patient learned to hold and appreciate many of her mother's emotions—guilt, shame, fear, love, and depression—while at the same time registering and making sense of how complicated the situation was. The key is not to blend the emotions but to put them together like puzzle pieces to reveal the big picture. My patient said, "She did what she did, and she loved me." In time, she was able to lay the foundation for a new construct about life by reestablishing who she is as a person (insightful and understanding) and who she is not (a perpetual victim).

Acceptance is achieved by shifting from the single-faceted first-person POV to the multifaceted third-person POV. If you understand something only one way, then you don't really understand it at all.

3. FORGIVENESS

You've already worked on forgiving yourself. Now experiment with forgiveness in a larger sense, with other people, circumstances, and persistent feelings.

Forgive and forget is *not* a healthy attitude. There's no point to trying to forget, since your unconscious can't and won't forget everything. All your emotions and memories are locked away in your mind's warehouses, and the more you try to suppress the bad stuff, the more it will seep out into your life in the form of unhealthy patterns and relationships. Insight is about shining a light into dark corners. Trying to forget or hide feelings is the opposite of that.

Forgive and remember is healthier, but there are traps in that mind-set too. Although it might seem smart to let go of resentment and anger while blaming the wrongdoer for creating the situation in the first place, *forgive and remember* is a recipe for grudge holding. As the saying goes, holding a grudge is like drinking poison and hoping the other person dies.

I urge patients to think of forgiving as another way to separate the problem from the person. Forgive or separate the negativity associated with your old story—including the bad actions of your parents and others—from your current existence. I'm not saying that you should let people who have harmed you off the hook. Some parents have committed acts that are unforgiveable. But you can endeavor to separate the resentment and bitterness you feel toward them from your heart now. Visualize all of the negative associations floating out of your body and into the ether. This is a wonderful, deep, and powerful experience, and one you'll want to repeat.

Forgiveness is the end-stage separation from past pain, the finale after detachment and acceptance. Your pathogenic belief is not your fault. You were a kid. You did what you had to do to feel safe and survive. Forgive yourself and forgive the people responsible for creating your destructive narrative in the first place. Let those negative associations go. You don't need them. They are not part of your new story. They need not be part of your new life.

WORKING THROUGH

Skylar

Skylar, the actor/escort with bulimia, doubted that therapy could help her at first, refusing to acknowledge that doing any emotional digging could be of value. But once she decided to try working through ("as an experiment, for material"), we were able to draw connections between her false truth and her current choices.

Her profession was being a "sugar baby" to much older men. The arrangement was that she'd have sex with them and then they would "gift" her jewelry or cash. Her emotions and memories were so locked in her unconscious, she'd forgotten that after her maternal grandfather abused her, he often gave her small presents or $10 bills. She told me, "He would say, 'Go buy some candy'; and now I'm a sugar baby." Her job wasn't, as she'd long insisted, just a way to pay her tuition and bills. There was more going on.

Skylar began to see that she needed to acknowledge these patterns and gain awareness about what was happening. Part of her was replaying the trauma she had been subjected to. An older man had made sexual advances on her, and now she was making herself available to other older men's sexual advances. Control mastery theory would hypothesize that she was testing her false truth over and over, confirming that she was right to believe all men were creeps and couldn't be trusted, while at the same time hoping, unconsciously, to disprove it by finding someone along the way who would prove to be decent and trustworthy.

Other things were going on too. I pointed out to her that being an escort and seeing it "as a job" enabled her to disconnect from her feelings so she didn't have to look harder at them. Her history of bulimia was likely symptomatic of the stress she either wasn't fully aware of or didn't know how to handle. Her false truth–related distrust was also why she was so selective about friendships and chose friends who shared her general contempt and cynicism.

Skylar connected the dots and saw how her ACE affected every aspect of her emotional, social, professional, and personal life, not to mention her health.

As part of working through, Skylar engaged in a confrontation with her parents about her grandfather's abuse. (In therapy terms, a confrontation is not an argument per se. It's speaking to the reality of a situation and a person's behavior.) Her father had no idea it was happening, but astonishingly her mother admitted that she'd also been abused at the same age by the same man, but couldn't allow herself to imagine that Skylar was being abused by him too.

Being able to talk about it, from both the mother's and the daughter's perspectives, was a huge breakthrough for the family. Although Skylar had some anger to work through regarding her mother, they both felt that the truth was better out than locked inside. Skylar also shared with her parents that she'd been working as an escort. It was a very rocky few months of revelations, but part of the Insight Cure is to be truthful and endure the pain now in order to have lasting relief and happiness later.

The Sharp Focus: You might have noticed a strong thread that runs through the three elements of change—empathy. In order to detach, accept, and forgive, you have to be able to see things from someone else's perspective and in effect put yourself in their shoes. Empathy can also be a tool for better understanding your own behavior, putting yourself in your own shoes. Remember, if you understand something from only one point of view, then you don't really understand it at all. By clueing in to the emotional aspects of cause and effect from multiple perspectives, you reevaluate your circumstances with emerging knowledge. The empathy you gain for yourself and other people will make insight shine even brighter.

CHANGE TOOL:

Empathy Map

In pre-insight days, you might have experienced a wide chasm between your intentions ("I'm not going to drink/cheat/crumble") and your actions (drinking, cheating, crumbling). With empathy you can boost insight and seal the gap between what you want, say, and do.

The idea of an empathy map was created by management consultant Scott Matthews for advertisers and marketers to get a better understanding of their clients' and customers' hopes, fears, and desires. The theory goes that if you can connect on a deep emotional level with consumers, you can sell more products.

In terms of personal development, an empathy map is a useful tool for empowerment and overcoming resistance to change. Because it's an intellectual exercise, you'll be able to use a third-person POV and work through with effective objectivity.

The map is a square with four quadrants: *thinking, seeing, feeling,* and *doing.* At the top of the map, write down a particular situation or relationship you'd like to explore. The subject line could be "my performance at work," "talking to strangers," or anything you want to analyze and get to the heart of. The *ideas* box is where you can jot down insights that come up. It's important to maintain that third-person detachment so you can notice false-truth connections but avoid judging or blaming yourself for making them.

Empathy Map

Subject Line: _____

| Thinking ——————————————————————————————————————— Seeing |
| | |
| Feeling ——————————————————————————————————————— Doing |

Ideas —————————————————————————————

In the *thinking* box, write keywords about what you're consciously thinking about the situation or person.

In *seeing*, write keywords about what you objectively observe.

In *feeling*, write down any emotions that come up, especially those that relate to the false truth. (A sample list of emotions can be found on page 62.)

In *doing*, write down recent behaviors and consistent past behavioral patterns.

For example, say your subject line is "Big, hairy fight with my husband about housecleaning." In *thinking*, you might write, "My husband is a lazy jerk who doesn't pull his weight around here." In *seeing*, you might write "dirty dishes, socks on the floor, husband on the couch." In *feeling*, you might write "unappreciated, angry, hurt, ignored." In *doing*, you might write "yelling, screaming, crying." In *ideas*, where you connect all of the above to your false truth, you might write, "Hubby activating 'no one cares' false truth. Reliving old story, 'No matter what I do, I won't get what I want,' zooming me right back to my childhood with my absent father and narcissistic mother."

For further insight into the situation, you could do an empathy map for your husband about what he is seeing and feeling, or ask him to do one for himself and then compare. Perhaps it'll come to light that your husband really is a lazy slob, or maybe he's just not sensitive enough to how you react when your "no one cares" button gets pushed. He probably has his own sensitivities that are being triggered as well.

By doing this exercise, you will quickly figure out what's really going on. Instead of exacerbating the "big, hairy fight" or getting into it the first place, you can use the tool to see things from all sides (including the inside), and open a dialogue that solves problems and strengthens the relationship.

Prove Yourself Wrong

The pre-insight life was, in part, defined by constantly striving to reconfirm, again and again, what you have always believed to be the truth (albeit the false truth). What makes the old story so tenacious is your innate human desire to "be right." You've always thought of yourself in a certain way and have expected things to unfold predictably. So unconsciously, you made damn sure they did. As painful as the outcomes might have been, you've taken some comfort in being right. People are amazing in their ability to find ways to validate their false truth. As a doctor, I just have to shake my head in amazement at how well people justify self-defeating behavior in order to match up their experiences with their expectations. A person suffering from paranoia who believes she's always in danger and that people are out to get her might put herself in dangerous situations that make her fears factually true.

As you work through with your shining light of insight and multifaceted third-person POV, set out to prove yourself *wrong*. You've always expected projects to crash and burn, and then they do, thanks to unconscious self-sabotage. That was then. From now on, change the outcome, even if you haven't yet been able to change the expectation.

Go ahead and assume the worst, but then do everything in your power to make the situation play out in *any other way* than what you expect.

Once, I had a patient with a slight limp from a long-ago car accident. He was very self-conscious about it and assumed no woman would want him. Before he went on dates, he wouldn't shower or shave. He wore stained, unflattering clothes and acted surly and dismissive. He used every weapon in his arsenal to ensure rejection. When he came to my office, he said, "See? I told you it would be a disaster. Why bother putting on cologne and a suit if I'm going to get shot down anyway?"

We discussed him trying a crazy experiment: On his next date, he would wear a clean suit, shave, smile, and be polite. Was being wrong a faint possibility? We'd have to see. Reluctantly, he agreed to try the experiment, just so he could prove *me* wrong. When he came in for his next session, he said, "Well, she friend-zoned me. But we had a nice night. I left the restaurant feeling pretty good about myself. Not a total success, but not a total disaster either." The date was proof that there are a million possible outcomes besides "disaster." Slowly, over the next month, his date expectations started to change.

You—not your false truth from childhood—get to decide how your life unfolds. Right now, all you have to do is accept that your assumptions about life might be bullshit. It helps to have a supportive cheerleader in your life—a therapist or friend—to encourage you to prove yourself wrong, but that's not required at this point. The thought alone ("Maybe my assumptions are wrong!") is compelling and can lead to real change. Just by connecting to the pages in this book, you can find the wherewithal and courage to set out to prove yourself wrong and reinforce the idea that, however tenacious it might be, your false truth is *not* your destiny.

Get excited about this! Build up some steam around it. Feel empowered by the idea. Stir it up, whoop it up. Do whatever you can to get pumped. Jumping jacks. A jig. You should feel psyched! This is going to be *good*.

WORKING THROUGH

Daria

Daria grew up in San Francisco and had a network of family and classmates there. Her chosen profession was film and television production, so it made perfect sense for her to move to LA. Although she told me repeatedly in therapy that her goal was to get into rewarding professional and personal relationships with people who wouldn't disappoint her, her move to a strange city was her way of validating her false truth that no one gets her and that she's on her own. LA was certainly a town bustling with career opportunities, but it also had a reputation for a culture of dog-eat-dog ambition and selfishness.

Sure enough, once Daria arrived in LA and tried to get jobs and make new friends, she was disappointed and alone again. Daria alienated people with her brutal honesty and too-probing questions. She would tell me she was trying to break through superficiality, but in effect she re-created the childhood feeling of being misunderstood. In every conversation, Daria confirmed her false truth. When she complained about these short-lived friendships and relationships with people who didn't really care about her, I asked her why she got into them in the first place.

"Because I hoped I'd be wrong," she said.

Hoping to be wrong and setting out to be wrong are completely different things. Hoping to be wrong is passive. She didn't change her behavior or way of thinking at all, and she re-created a situation where she'd be right. If she had set out to be wrong, she would have experimented with changing her behavior to guarantee a different outcome.

In therapy, Daria learned to adopt a mentality of reality and to ask herself, "What do I expect versus what is actually happening?" and "What has this person actually done to earn my trust or distrust?" She learned to let someone earn her trust gradually over time by communicating between dates, following through, admitting mistakes, taking responsibility, and taking care. She learned to watch out for people who made big promises that didn't materialize.

The Sharp Focus: We are drawing clear distinctions between your pre- and post-insight life in this step, working through how things used to be and seeing how they can and will be. In your pre-insight days, you might have just gone along with something you knew would end badly to enjoy the dubious pleasure of being right. The post-insight you, however, won't passively allow your life to proceed as it always has. Snafus are times you actively make expectations come to fruition. Instead, shine the light on your choices and say, "What am I expecting to happen? What other outcomes are possible? What changes can I make in what I ordinarily do that will prove me wrong?" Be conscious about what you are doing and thinking, and try to put something new into the world. Apply this hugely proactive thinking and prepare positively to prove yourself wrong.

How to Make Change

Working through is an ongoing process of seeing the insight-illuminated world with new eyes. Once people realize "Wow, I actually constructed some of my problems for myself in order to prove myself right," they start to believe their life doesn't have to be the way it has been. The false truth loses its grip, and they take control of their lives.

It's a major breakthrough. In therapy, patients' eyes light up. Excitement might be tempered by what I call *fish-out-of-water fears*. They've been seeing and doing things a certain way for their whole lives. And now they're supposed to stop being fish and become birds? How will they learn to fly and breathe air? Swimming and water is all they know. Flying might feel awkward at first. But soon enough it'll feel as if you were born with wings.

Take a moment to appreciate how many changes you have already made on this journey and to tally the emotional skills you've acquired, like detachment, acceptance, forgiveness, and empathy. You've learned that being right can be wrong and that resistances can be overcome. You are already changing and are now ready to widen your stride and take faster, bigger steps.

Contemplating a new life in a new world can be terrifying. Combat fear by remembering that you've changed in the past, in childhood, when your false truth was formed and you maladapted to a new reality. Now you'll adapt again, but in a positive and healthy way, armed with adult understanding and faith that you can write a new story and have a happy, successful life today and in the future.

CHANGE STARTER #1: REVIEW SITUATIONS

Accelerate the shift by bringing your new awareness into familiar situations and making an effort to do things differently. Say, for example, you had a meltdown at work last week. The boss called you in to talk about fixing a project. Besides being bummed about disappointing the boss and having to redo the job, you felt *crushed*.

The intense emotion related to your pathogenic belief, "It doesn't matter how hard I try, I always fall short."

The worse you feel, the more likely your reaction has to do with your false truth.

When you realize you're having an intense reaction, stop what you're doing and ask, "How does this situation conform to or reiterate something I've always known to be true? To what extent did I make this happen to prove my false truth right? Is this a pattern I'm all too familiar with?"

If you get a powerful "oh shit!" sinking clarity, great. As soon as you see the connection, work it through. Take five minutes to bring awareness to the situation. And then make an effort to prove yourself wrong by doing things differently.

This psychological process can be called *check yourself before you wreck yourself.* (If only that phrase appeared in the *Diagnostic and Statistical Manual of Mental Disorders!*) Reviewing the situation and stopping a downward spiral before it happens will give you a sense of control. It's the best way I've found to break bad habits.

You're up against the tremendous pull of human nature to replay the same tune, over and over and over again. But you can step away from something you've been doing forever and take control.

If you've always believed that you could never do an A-plus job on anything, you might, without really noticing it, cut corners or procrastinate. As a result, the boss tells you that your project could have been better, and you feel miserable. You weren't trying to make yourself miserable, but you did anyway. Being a passive self-saboteur is not fun. However, now that you know what you've been doing, you can start the next project earlier and avoid the shortcuts.

WORKING THROUGH

Larry

Larry felt inadequate in the professional realm, so he married a workhorse, a wildly successful woman, a star. It made sense to him on a few levels. Consciously, as a perpetual underachiever, he knew he wouldn't make enough money for the kind of life he dreamed of, so he found a wife who could provide for him. Unconsciously, he chose a partner who would be a constant reinforcement of the false truth that he's not good enough. His wife's very existence confirmed his sense of inadequacy.

Human nature truly is spectacularly complex. In Larry's choice of a partner, he both championed and punished himself. He made a rational, useful choice *and* reinforced his painful false truth in one decision.

For Larry to break his pattern of procrastination, we discussed setting a task for him to complete on time. It had to be job-related, since work was his sensitive area. He would have to fully commit to it. And he would have to finish strong. I suggested he focus right from the beginning on how he hoped the project would end.

He decided that the project would be a business consultation, something he was familiar with. To commit to it, he put the date on the calendar for the consultation, which was in a month, and he set daily deadlines to meet leading up to the big day. It was important for him to be able to look at that calendar and see every single thing he'd have to do from beginning to end.

Every week at our sessions, we discussed how he felt as he met his daily deadlines. When procrastination (the manifestation of his false truth) crept in, he beat it by saying, "Procrastination is how I proved myself right. I'm going to prove myself wrong this time."

On occasion he showed up late for our appointments or "plain forgot." I interpreted this as him working against himself, undermining his interest in making important changes happen. His procrastination or not showing up for therapy wasn't laziness at all. It was an active process designed to interfere. I gave him credit for that and he vowed to more aggressively manage his time and follow through.

In the end, he went to that consultation better prepared than he'd ever been before—and he got hired. But the real victories for him were his plan coming to fruition, newly believing that inadequacy didn't have to be his reality, and having the courage to break new ground in his experience of living. It does indeed take courage.

CHANGE STARTER #2: REASSESS RELATIONSHIPS

Along with looking more closely at familiar situations, work through your relationships too. Take an objective look at your friendships. Do they prove your false truth right? If a friendship triggers feelings of inadequacy, worthlessness, neediness, or desperation, ask yourself, "Why am I in it if it makes me feel bad? Does it have to be like this? Can it be different?"

As you assess your relationships, be aware that some will grow stronger, some will change, and some will have to be sacrificed. In many cases, friends and colleagues will be happy for you as you grow in positive new ways. They'll tolerate the changes you're making, and the relationships will be flexible enough to continue into the future. Some friends might even be inspired to flip the insight switch for themselves, and you'll grow and evolve together.

And other relationships? They won't survive, and good riddance. There's an old saying that people are in your life for a reason, a season, or a lifetime. Some friendships fit your false truth and were part of an unhealthy unconscious pattern. The critical boyfriends, the emotional vampires, the users, the bullies—all of these people had their reason and their season. But unless they are supportive of the changes you need to make, you're going to have to move on from them.

WORKING THROUGH

Bobby

Bobby was blindly trusting, and he got into trouble as a result. When a friend betrayed him, he never saw it coming. His old story, "If I respect and love people, they'll love me back," came from growing up with bullying brothers, a belittling father, and an absent mother. Bobby lived by the Beatles assumption that "love is all you need." In reality, some bad people take advantage of blind trust. In fact, they seek out kind hearts like Bobby for that purpose.

Bobby had to ready himself to replace the "sustaining loyalties" that he granted people with "situational" or "conditional" loyalties.

We discussed his need to judge people by their actions and how to guard himself against users. "Someone is only good for you as long as they're good for you and are working to prove it," I said.

"What about giving people the benefit of the doubt?" he asked.

"The benefit of the doubt almost lost you your business."

I guided Bobby to try to separate another false truth, "I'm lovable with the right people," from nefarious business practices.

Bobby's task was seeing the world from a third-person POV. In the music business, he couldn't survive by assuming everyone had a conscience and a giving nature. Bobby had to learn to say, "This friendship or partnership is only good when it's good for *me*. It's not selfish to stop people from ripping me off."

It wasn't easy for Bobby to objectively evaluate people and to feel better about himself for doing it. What he noticed almost immediately was that his friendships were all casual. He would show up at an event or concert and say "hey" to his friends, and then they'd drift away. He'd wanted to believe that those people really loved him and that they were there for him in the way he would be for them. "I've been living in a one-sided world," he told me. "When I looked at my life from behind the camera, all I saw was my attempt to make people like me and their being turned off or taking advantage of my neediness."

Tearing the blinders off might hurt, but it will eventually help you grow stronger and build new, healthier relationships.

Change Starter #3: Share Your Journey

If you haven't already, it's appropriate and advisable to start discussing your journey with someone else at this point. Talking about it might bring deeper clarity and insight. I call it the *talking through* of *working through*. You're not looking for advice or validation, but just giving yourself the opportunity to get used to saying your new truth out loud.

When you choose this person, choose wisely. Steer clear of major conversations with those closest to you. You're still in the process of figuring out how they may or may not play a role in your false-truth scripts. You don't know how all the changes you're experiencing will affect those relationships. Opening up to someone who would prefer you to stay stuck might cause unnecessary stress and anxiety that will slow your growth.

Who you should not share your journey with (yet):

- Your spouse, girlfriend, boyfriend, or exes. It's too risky, too close.

- Your boss, employees, or colleagues. Don't bring emotional issues to work.

- Your children, even if they are supportive adults. It's not appropriate to burden them with your problems.

- Your children's friends' parents. This is also inappropriate and could needlessly expose your children to gossip and harm.

- Your best friends. You are in the thick of looking at which of your friendships are supportive and healthy and which are reinforcing your false truth. It's better to wait before confiding in anyone very close to you yet.

- Your parents. God, no! That's like hiking in a minefield.

- Your siblings. They might have had a completely different experience of childhood and could inadvertently try to discount your insight.

- Narrow-minded people. You have to be careful to avoid picking a narrow-minded person who makes the same mistakes over and over again or is currently in her own crisis. You might look at her and think, "But she'd benefit from this process too!" That might be true, and you can give her a copy of *The Insight Cure* later and talk about how it worked out for you. But for now, steer clear. You have your own path.

Instead, talk to low-stakes people in your life, casual or inconsequential connections with no currency in your life right now.

Who you should share with:

- A person on the periphery of your life who seems accepting and lives in the present.

- A spiritual advisor who can listen without injecting doctrine into your explorations and experiences.

- Someone you see only casually. I opened up to the concierge at my condo building. We made small talk and I had grown to like him a lot. One day, I commented on something I'd been worried about— making the deadline for this book, actually!—and he said, "Don't worry too much, Doc. Just keep going. You'll get there." It was a generic encouragement, but those few sentences on my way out the door made me feel so much better. It validated my fears and helped me work through them.

- A random person with a few degrees of separation from your life, like a person at a dinner party who you probably won't see again for a long while.

- An old friend you haven't spoken to in years but trust. Facebook makes it easy to find them, and then in a "catching up after all these years" conversation, say, "I've been thinking a lot about my past lately and have realized some important things I'm trying to work through." This may be your best option, actually!

- A complete stranger! The lowest stakes possible. A willing seatmate on a long flight can be a benign sounding board. Perhaps starting with a short flight would be better though. It can start with the most basic question: "Where did you grow up?" Let him talk for a while, and then when it's your turn, go where you need to go.

Whoever you share with, keep it clear, short, and simple. I have found that when you speak from the heart, people respond in kind. "I used to think I was a loser, but now I see that it was only a story I told myself" is as simple and profound as it gets. People might get it and nod approvingly. They might give you the side-eye and judge you too. Some people are more open to these kinds of conversations than others.

An old expression from the '60s was *Hey, man, don't lay your trip on me.* If someone reacts strongly to your confidences, it's likely she is laying her trip—her projected expectations about the world—on you. Unless she happens to be a professional advice-giver on duty, you can bet she will give you the advice that *she* wants to hear.

So if you let someone know what you're doing and he looks at you funny, it's quite healthy to say to yourself, "That's his problem," and go elsewhere. Importantly, please remember that you're not looking for advice or validation. You are just sharing and getting comfortable talking about this stuff.

CHANGE TOOL:

The Changing Scale

How do you know if any of this reviewing and assessing is doing anything? You can actually track real change on a scale. The further you go, the deeper the change will be, and the more natural and healthy it will feel. Professor of psychology at the University of Rhode Island James O. Prochaska, along with his colleague Carlo DiClemente, developed the transtheoretical model, otherwise known as the *stages of change*, in the 1970s, and wrote about it in *Changing for Good*. (For more info, see page 236.)

According to Prochaska, change is a progression with six distinct stages:

1. **Pre-contemplation:** A person isn't ready to change and doesn't believe change is necessary. For example, a smoker loves his cigarettes and willfully ignores health warnings.

2. **Contemplation:** A person is getting ready to change and realizes that it might be necessary. The smoker can't ignore the warnings anymore and is psyching himself up to quit.

3. **Preparation:** A person is ready to change and intends to do it very soon, or is taking preliminary steps already. The smoker might research nicotine gum, patches, or the effectiveness of going cold turkey.

4. **Action:** A person is changing his old behavior and adopting new behaviors. The smoker quits or is systematically reducing his daily cigarette breaks.

5. **Maintenance:** A person is sticking with new behaviors for at least six months and making sure he doesn't fall back into old habits. The smoker has completely stopped and is doing things to avoid being around temptation.

6. **Termination:** A person has changed so completely, he's not even tempted to go back to the way things were. The smoker is so off cigarettes, he's disgusted by the smell.

Prochaska didn't call relapsing a stage but described it as something that can always happen during *action* or *maintenance*. If a relapse does occur, the smoker, for example, would just revert back to the *action* stage and begin the progression anew.

I devised a scale of my own, the Changing Scale, that I use in my practice to assess where patients are in their journey to change.

1. **Pre-change.** When you know you're unhappy but don't know why.

2. **Preparation.** You learn about the unconscious and the existence of a false truth that is controlling you; then you figure out what it is and how it got there.

3. **Motion.** You reflect on the false truth and work it through in your past and present. To solidify insights, you take a new look at where you are, what you're doing, and with whom you're associating. By talking about your process with select confidants, you are making a commitment to it and making it more real.

4. **Perpetual motion.** Insight is sufficiently worked through and you begin to build a new identity based on strengths and virtues, testing the new narrative repeatedly until any vestiges of the old you are irrelevant or gone.

5. **Post-change.** You are a new person. And you will continue to be, as you go forward through life's ups and downs.

The Sharp Focus: I've been saying throughout the process that change is difficult, given how entrenched your false truth is. But it is not impossible. Now that you have done the hard work of excavating the false truth, you've gained insight and reflected about how the false truth has affected your life, and you've really worked it through and prepared yourself by reviewing and assessing your current existence, you are ready to enact major change. At this point, change is not only possible, it's inevitable. Stay present and keep going.

Gut Check

As you prepare to leap into change, you might feel:

Astonishment. As you work through the false truth and learn to understand things from multiple perspectives, you will probably be astonished by what you perceive. Astonishment might be accompanied by sadness or anger, but I'll ask you to forgive those negative associations and focus instead on the enormity of what you've discovered.

Eager. As you imagine yourself as a hero on a journey inward and into an extraordinary new world, you are probably chomping at the bit to get moving. Eager patients have to be reminded to take this journey one step at a time. It's not a race; it's a process, with each part building on the next. It's great to feel excited and to keep that energy up, just as long as you also stay mindful about what you're doing.

Intimidated. I've asked a lot of you in this step, to look at everything with new eyes, to teach yourself objectivity, to be more empathetic and see things from multiple angles. You might feel those fish-out-of-water fears and doubt that you will be able to breathe outside the stagnant pond that has been your life for so long. I've also asked you to trust in the process of turning your life, thoughts, and sense of self inside out. Fish can be birds. Birds can be dragons. You can be whoever you can imagine. Stay in touch with your authentic self and dream big.

STEP SIX

BUILDING
A NEW STORY

Now that you have exposed your old story and are deep in the ongoing process of working it through, the time has finally come for you to create a new narrative for the rest of your life.

I'd like to take a moment to explain exactly what that means.

In popular culture, you often hear about "manifesting" your dreams, the idea that if you tell yourself a story such as, "I'm going to be rich and famous!" or "I'm going to live in a mansion and drive a Mercedes!" you can make it come true. The trick, or "the secret," supposedly is to keep a picture of the Mercedes in your head or on a vision board, and someday soon a new car will somehow drive its way into your life.

In my practice, my goal is not to make fairytales come true by magic. I help people who are suffering find a new focus, a new sense of self—their authentic self—and navigate through the real world with inner strength. For some, that might mean quantifiable professional success. For others, it might be forming close, intimate, trusting relationships. It might be inner calm and tranquility. I'm not saying a new Mercedes is not in your future. It very well might be. But fantasy fulfillment about material possessions isn't relevant to the Insight Cure. The work you're doing in this book is about being happy with who you are and feeling confident every time you walk out the door.

(FYI: It's not emotionally healthy to define yourself by the car you drive.)

By now, you've done a lot of emotional heavy lifting. The work has made you feel lighter. You've dropped the chains that you've carried since childhood. Now you're ready to create a new narrative for your insightful existence. You are the main character in the story of your life, and as you recall from the hero's journey, you have left former fears and limitations behind. You've entered the unknown extraordinary world, where you will be tested and transformed.

If you *hadn't* unlocked your unconscious false truth and unblocked your true self, you could have continued to live according to the old story. But you *have* done the work, and now you are embarking on a new life as a new person, living a different story than the familiar unhealthy one.

Some physicists say that every moment exists forever and will continue to exist forever. But if you are brave enough to believe your real truth, you can step away from that false-truth moment and into another moment that exists forever. A better moment. I believe this very deeply.

Now that you are lit up from the inside with insight, you can see paths that were previously hidden. You have clarity about relationships (some that might need to end), your work style, and how you react to minor and major stressors. Everything that insight has revealed to you will change the direction of your life as you move forward.

YOUR NEW NARRATIVE OF CONFIDENCE, STRENGTH, AND HAPPINESS IS INEVITABLE.

To prepare for the seismic shifts ahead, refocus the insight microscope yet again. Turn the dial another tick to get a clearer, closer, deeper look at who you are as you evolve. Reach down deep, and reach outward at the same time. What are your values? What are your strengths? What are you good at? What do you have to offer other people and the whole world?

For any story to be authentic, it has to be based on essential real truths. The life you lived before wasn't authentic; it was based on a childhood false truth of pain and difficulty. You were handicapped by it, blinded. Your worldview was hijacked. The life you create now will be based on your adult reality of insight, mindfulness, empathy, confidence, and strength, in glorious 3-D. You can move through the world in every direction and dimension with reclaimed authenticity and strength.

You've got a lot going for you, and it will all be useful in your new narrative of confidence and trust, closeness and love, success and happiness.

Showing Up Is Eighty Percent of Identity

It is often said that eighty percent of life is showing up.

As you create a new identity based on who you are becoming, it's wise to remember that insight requires vigilance. Your old narrative was a well-trodden path that would be only too easy to go back to as you begin to pave a new one. To avoid that, be mindful and present about your progress in the Insight Cure; remember how far you've come to get away from old, bad habits and to create a new life and identity for yourself. To turn insight into lasting change, stay vigilant about your commitment. Strive to understand what's going on in your head and heart. Keep examining and assessing yourself, situations, and relationships. The opposite of showing up is being on automatic pilot. Don't do that for a second. Keep your hands on the wheel, eyes on the road, and mind in the moment.

One time, when I was trying to change my life, I quite literally got stuck because I didn't show up.

I'd finished my residency training in San Francisco and had started to consider where to look for a position as an attending physician. Before returning to Boston, I applied at neighboring Stanford University. I arrived early and was guided into a professor's office to wait for my interviews. It happened to be the office of Irvin Yalom, a famous psychiatrist and fantastic writer whose novels like *Love's Executioner* and textbooks on existential psychotherapy were on my bookshelves at home. In a nutshell he said that to be well-adjusted, you had to get in the ring and grapple with some truths about life, such as "life is unfair" and "we all die." He postulated that if you don't come to terms with those basic realities, you'll never be happy.

I was so overwhelmed to be sitting there in Yalom's office among all his books and papers. I drifted into a fantasy about already being one of the club in that special place. Unfortunately, I took that "already there" feeling right into the interview. I was dazzled into blindness and basically forgot to show up. I didn't deliver my new narrative in the terms we are speaking of here. I didn't articulate what I could bring to the position, what my vision was, or how I would indeed be a great match for what they needed. I felt worthy—though perhaps too worthy as a freshly minted attending physician speaking with senior faculty about an important position in their ranks.

The interviewers must have been surprised when I didn't make a case for myself or try to impress them with my own point of view, and needless to say, I didn't get the position. The chairman of the department said to me later, "Sharpie, come back when you've developed more of a shtick."

So here's the lesson: Do *not* forget to show up for yourself. Yes, you are worthy—*and* you have to make the case for yourself when it counts—*and* it almost always counts.

In some regard, most of us have been dazzled blind by our old stories and false beliefs, and as a result, we don't show up for life. We don't get our point across. And we don't wind up where we hope to be.

As you create your new narrative based on essential real truths about who you really are, make this a recurring line of your story:

"I am vigilant about taking a close, clear look at myself and my actions. I don't fall back into blindness and old habits. I show up."

Narrative Essentials

Narrative therapy (NT) was formulated in the 1970s and '80s by two social workers, Australian Michael White and New Zealander David Epston. (For more about NT, see page 233.) It's all about identity. In NT, the patient works with a therapist to describe her values and skills. These attributes are components of identity. Once a composite of identity is drawn, the patient steps into this composite character, a person who has a lot going for her, with many talents and abilities to share and use as she moves through life.

To reinforce this identity, or narrative, the patient puts on the hat of a psyche detective and "investigates" times in the past when she exhibited and actually used the strengths and virtues that are the components of her identity. For example, if one of your strengths is generosity, when have you been benevolent before? If your new identity includes the skill of leadership, when have you inspired others to action before? By investigating the past and compiling evidence that your strength is real, you will believe that your new narrative is your true identity. Here's an interesting finding: If your narrative traits include qualities that benefit others, your new narrative is more likely to solidify. This harkens back to Campbell's and Vogler's versions of the hero's journey. The journey isn't complete until the hero returns home with the "boon" to share with the whole family, community, and world.

Of course, not all the components of one's identity are positive or benevolent. The first step at Alcoholics Anonymous is to identify yourself as an addict. However, NT is where we learn the truth that the problem is not the person. The person is not the problem. The problem is the problem. The person is the person.

Healing and happiness lie in separating negatives from a positive identity. Instead of saying, "Hello, my name is Adam. I'm an alcoholic," the NT version of AA's first step would be saying, "Hello, my name is Adam. I'm a person with an addiction to alcohol." The difference is subtle but significant. By hitting the core concept—you are not your problem—over and over again, you are less likely to define yourself by your problems.

NT is particularly effective in couples' therapy. Ordinarily, in a regular talk therapy session, one person might say, "When you do *x*, it makes me feel *y*," which can lead to defensiveness and accusations that are not productive. However, if someone says, "When you do *x*, the story I make up in my head about what's going on is *y*," the other person will not feel attacked and they can get to the heart of what's really going on.

For example, a husband says, "When you reject me sexually, the story I make up in my head about what's going on is that I'm disgusting to you, unlovable, and that you married me for my money." The wife can't diminish the story in his head by saying it doesn't exist or that it's ridiculous. It does exist. It is his reality. And it has to be addressed. It's very powerful to see how NT opens the door for honesty, vulnerability, and compassion.

In my work with athletes, we have used NT to overcome anxiety. For them, it's about replacing one story ("I'm going to come in dead last and humiliate myself!") with another clear, close focus on what will happen, incorporating the necessary element of success. So a hurdler tells the story in his head, "I'm going to come off the blocks strong, and when I come to the first gate, I will kick my leg up and over clean. Then I'm going to land well and run fast to the next hurdle, just like I have a thousand times before . . ." and so on. Narrative therapy is the story of how he prepares, how he draws a line between narration and actualization. Words become the basis for how he will, literally, propel himself forward successfully. It's not magic or fantasy. It's proving to yourself that you have a strong foundation for success.

As long as insight has been deeply felt, you won't have trouble authenticating the new story in your head, heart, and gut. One of my mentors explained NT as a kind of self-coaching. What does a coach do? She gives her team what it needs to succeed by unlocking the talent and confidence that already exists within each member. The self-esteem you need is already in you. You don't have to import it from someone or something else to be healthy. Just unblock what's already there by putting the words and images in your head: "**I am capable. I am strong. I can do it.**"

Your false truth and old narrative—the story in your head—used to be your reality. It was a story that was constructed to make you feel safe when you were very young. Now you can start over with the story of yourself that accounts for everything you think and feel *minus the false truth*. If you are not "a loser," "unlovable," or "worthless," then who are you? Reconsider yourself and bravely have faith that you are someone else, someone who is in the process of proving a new story based on strength, based on what is actually happening.

If your old story was "I'm a screwup," the new story becomes, "**I used to be attached to the idea that I was a screwup, but I'm not attached to that now. I don't know what's going to happen, but I'm going to use my positive identity to be good and do good for myself and others.**"

The Sharp Focus: Karen Blixen, aka Isak Dinesen, author of *Out of Africa*, once said, "All sorrows can be borne if you put them into a story or tell a story about them." This idea is central to narrative therapy. By putting something—in this case, your character and life—in the form of a story, you can understand it and better tolerate any difficult emotions around it. You've already been doing this with the third-person POV. By stepping alongside yourself and becoming an observer or creator of yourself and your life, you have greater control.

CREATING A NEW NARRATIVE

Skylar

Working as an "sugar baby" escort for much older men and going on auditions where she was scrutinized about her looks only served to reinforce Skylar's false truth, that all men (and many women) were creeps and not to be trusted. She'd had her guard up against human connection for so long she couldn't put it down. Until therapy, that shield worked both ways. No one got past it to access her heart. And she didn't allow herself to delve into her past or the deeper emotions and memories that created the global distrust to begin with, namely, emotions and memories about her grandfather's sexual abuse.

In Skylar's case, where she was reliving her trauma in a very direct sense, she would have to make big changes in the circumstances of her life in order to build a new narrative for herself. Being an escort was no longer an option. Living in LA and trying to be an actor was not an option. Skylar had to end her false-truth confirming employment and dreams.

Along with acting lessons, Skylar had been taking some writing workshops. We discussed her going back to school to hone her skills. She'd saved up a lot of money and could make it happen. Within a few months, Skylar was accepted into a masters of fine arts program in Chicago and moved across the country.

As a new Chicagoan, Skylar could reinvent and redefine herself easily. She decided to concentrate on her strengths of creativity, curiosity, open-mindedness, and love of learning as she embarked on her life as a full-time graduate student and essayist. "It really feels like a fresh start," she said. "I don't have anything to be ashamed of, and I have no regrets. Being a sugar baby paid for college. But now I see that the behavior was keeping me locked in a toxic mind-set and caused a lot of unhealthy stress." Instead of reliving her trauma, Skylar started writing about it, and the difference in her attitude about life was enormous. She now had control of her old story while building a new one.

NARRATIVE TOOL:

Identify Your Strengths

I've been talking about defining yourself by your virtues and strengths. You have a long list to choose from. In *Character Strengths and Virtues,* psychologists Christopher Peterson and Martin Seligman classified six *core virtues* and the *character strengths* that fall under each virtue category.

As you'll see below, these skills and traits come up again and again in the world of mental and emotional health, from Erikson's stages of development to Maslow's hierarchy of needs to Campbell's hero's journey. In your own life, on the basis of your psychology and heredity, some of these strengths will be greater than others. Although each one is admirable, they're not all requirements for happiness and well-being.

Which virtues and strengths in the list below fit you? What are you really good at? What have you thought of as your special skills, gifts, or talents? As you build your post-insight life and identity, you will be emphasizing and playing to these positive attributes.

Circle your virtues (below, in **bold**) and strengths (below, in *italics*):

Wisdom

Creativity. Thinking and producing creatively and conceptually.

Curiosity. Exploring and discovering your interests with enthusiasm.

Open-mindedness. Looking at things from all sides.

Love of learning. Pursuing education and skill mastery for the pleasure of it.

Perspective. Making sense of the world and sharing your ideas with others.

Courage

Bravery. Daring to follow your heart, and not shying away from danger or pain.

Persistence. Sticking with something until it's achieved.

Integrity. Taking responsibility for who you are and what you do.

Vitality. Bursting with life force, energy, and enthusiasm.

Humanity

Love. Having mutually trusting and nurturing relationships with family, friends, and romantic partners.

Kindness. Being generous and nice to others.

Social intelligence. Having awareness about why other people do, say, and feel things.

Justice

Teamwork. Working well in a group.

Fairness. Being judicious and democratic in your dealings with others and not letting bias dictate your reasoning.

Leadership. Inspiring others to do their best work and winning their trust.

Temperance

Forgiveness and mercy. Accepting other people's flaws, forgiving their wrongdoings, and feeling compassion.

Humility and modesty. Not bragging about your accomplishments, and remembering that you're a person just like everyone else.

Prudence. Not rushing in or saying things without careful consideration.

Self-control. Having discipline, not giving in to desires, and tempering your feelings.

Transcendence

Appreciation of beauty and excellence. Being a true fan and admirer of natural beauty, human skill, and the little things in life.

Gratitude. Saying thank you for the good in your life.

Hope. Having faith that things will work out in the end.

Humor. Laughing a lot, smiling, cracking jokes, and always looking on the bright side of life.

Spirituality. Believing in a higher power and having clear ideas about the meaning of life.

Now that you have your list of strengths and virtues, use the power of language to remind yourself of who you are. Fill in the blanks in the following sentences and speak them out loud as part of the story about who you are, and what you, as a strong person, want and can achieve.

"I am _____, _____, _____, _____ and _____."

I am a person who deeply cares about _____, _____, and _____.

Right now, I am looking for a _____.

Ultimately, I want _____.

Build out some of your ideas about your goals by categorizing them in terms of things you'd like to accomplish this year, this month, this week, and today.

Yearly goals are medium or long term, the things you can work toward, define, and imagine how they might manifest concretely over the course of 365 days.

Monthly goals are derivatives of yearly goals. What do you need to accomplish this month and in the months ahead in service of your long-term goals?

Weekly goals are derivations of monthly goals. Identify what you would need to accomplish by the end of this week, and the week ahead, to realize your monthly goals.

Daily goals are the small steps you would need to put on your to-do list for today and tomorrow to complete your weekly goals.

For example, if your yearly goal is "Have a more varied and fulfilling social life," your monthly goal might be to be a part of a group interested in some activity that you are or could be interested in. Your weekly goal could be to identify a few decent options for yourself, say a riding group, a book group, going hiking with some people, or volunteering once a week at a charity.

Your goal for tomorrow then would be to pick up the phone or sign up online, or to actually go to a gathering.

Don't overreach though. It's not that you don't have the capacity to do more and reach further. It's that success builds on success. You are newly in touch with your sense of empowerment. Be careful with your precious self and let your accomplishments accrue. Remember to put yourself to work toward these well-defined ends. Bring your best game by articulating the case for yourself and proving your self-efficacy—your new narrative—first in your mind, then outwardly as need be.

The Sharp Focus: Throughout the process of building a real-truth identity and setting long- and short-term goals, it's possible to feel overwhelmed by how huge a change you're making. Stay centered with the words *strength* and *confidence*. It's all about using strengths to build confidence. With confidence, you will have better work habits, and you'll be less reactive and defensive in interpersonal relationships. In shaky moments, remember your strengths. What are they? Say the words out loud.

Exceptions That Change the Rules

By luck or intention, at various times in the past you broke through your false truth. During those glimmers, you overcame it and lived a different way.

Search your memory for that great job you lucked into or managed to land that was a perfect fit. Recall a relationship that was mutually trusting, affectionate, and supportive, or a particular friendship that was fun and nurturing. The exceptional—meaning *rare* as well as *awesome*—experience was a time in the past when you felt safe and happy, when your false truth did not sabotage you. You might have had many exceptional experiences or only a few. In most cases, they do tend to be temporary. The tenacity of the false truth is just too powerful for non-insightful people to overcome. Your attachment to the old story forced you to prove yourself right and damage or dismantle that good thing in your life (as in, "I knew it was too good to be true"). Now that you have insight and are vigilantly striving to show up and prove your false truth wrong, your unconscious narrative will not control your behavior. What used to be glimmers of happiness and confidence can become your everyday reality.

Spend some time during your weekly half-hour reflection sessions to recall exceptional experiences from the past. In doing so, you will (1) prove you have (and have always had) the capacity to be happy and (2) remember the tenacity of the false truth that you have to vigilantly refute. You used to be attached to it, but you are no longer controlled by it. You can be happy, and continue to be happy, without feeling an unconscious need to throw a monkey wrench into the works.

YOU ARE IN THE THROES OF MAKING A HUGE ATTITUDINAL SHIFT. THE NEW NARRATIVE REALLY IS A NEW LEASE ON LIFE.

As patients embark on exploring a new positive identity, I always tell them that they're not starting from scratch. There have been times when their finest qualities have dominated. According to control mastery theory, you've *always* been testing out alternatives to the old story in little ways that feel safe, even if these experiences didn't last or amount to much. But the fact is, there were times when you were able to see yourself in a different way, with a particular person or in a certain situation.

I remember when I was in high school, I was a solid B-plus/A-minus student. I did well and was happy with my grades, but I was very aware I wasn't at the top. Other kids got straight A's and didn't seem to work that hard to get them. My grandfather, a quiet whiz at all things academic, was like them. I admired him, but I couldn't relate to his effortless aptitude. I assumed I wasn't like him or my overachieving peers and that my marks were the best I could do.

I walked into advanced calculus with that assumption firmly in place. The teacher was this lovable guy, really warm and caring with thick coke-bottle glasses. I went to an all-boys' school, with coat-and-tie uniforms, where we had to call every teacher "Master." So this poor teacher with a great New England name, Nathaniel Bates, was called "Master Bates" dozens of times a day. It was a riot every single time.

So Master Bates was a nice, really smart guy who for some reason thought I was a nice, really smart kid. He believed in my math mind and told me I was doing really well, even when I messed up on my first tries at the problem sets. He encouraged me to do better than I normally would, or could, have. He also pushed me: "By failing to prepare, Sharp," he warned me, "you are preparing to fail."

I got an A in the class.

His influence didn't suddenly transform me into one of those effortless straight-A kids, or into my grandfather for that matter. But it was proof that I could do better than I normally did. To use control mastery terms, I was testing a new sense of self, even though I wasn't able to maintain it across the board. Master Bates's belief in me, together with his nonthreatening relatability, combined to show me new things about myself that I wasn't sure about. I was inspired to do—and more importantly, be—better than I expected.

The exceptional experiences *change* the rules. They prove that you can be better than you'd previously imagined.

The new rules to go with your new narrative are:

1. You are not your false truth.

2. Your old story is not the only story.

3. You have already lived an alternative reality.

4. You can author a new narrative based on what you have already experienced to be true about your best self.

The new narrative mantra would be "**I have already experienced life as my best self, and I will use these exceptional experiences to reinforce the person I am becoming and as a guide for future interactions to play out in a positive way.**"

CREATING A NEW NARRATIVE

Carrie

At age five, Carrie developed the false truth that if she didn't appear strong, her entire world would crumble. As a result, adult Carrie was weakened by the fear of appearing weak. When her veneer of strength was challenged, she was overwhelmed by the internal conflict and either crumbled or shut down. I asked her to think of *any* times in her past when facing a challenge hadn't paralyzed her.

"During my semester abroad in college, I went to Thailand to teach girls about sexual education," she said. "On our first weekend in Chiang Mai, my friends and I went to this sprawling, crowded flea market that's only open at night. I got separated from my friends. I didn't speak Thai or know where I was in relation to our hostel. I was still jet-lagged and disoriented from the long trip. Basically, I was completely lost and should have felt terrified and overwhelmed. There was a moment of panic when I realized my friends weren't in sight. But then I just started wandering through the stalls, taking in the sights, having some dumplings, and shopping. I enjoyed myself and eventually found my way back to the hostel. I coped. And I felt very proud of myself."

We talked about why she didn't crumble that time. "I couldn't. It wasn't an option," she said. "I had to deal."

"It *was* an option," I reframed for her. "And you chose not to crumble, Carrie. You rallied. That isn't always what you expect from yourself, but you do have the strength to rally. You are that woman too."

Carrie realized that usually when she crumbled under stress, it was over something relatively minor. But when her father died, she was able to be strong. When she was lost in a foreign city, she coped. Carrie came to see that she allowed herself to fall apart only when it was safe to do so. Having made this discovery, she could summon her inner strength at will since she knew it was there.

Her new narrative became **"I used to be someone who let little things get to me, but I'm not attached to that anymore. Even if I feel weak, I can still be strong and cope."**

NARRATIVE TOOL:

Negative Assumptions versus Positive Intentions

Pre-insight, your anticipation of negative outcomes became a self-fulfilling prophecy that perpetuated itself. You were locked in a cycle of assumptions turning into predictions, which impacted your actions and provided confirmation that your original negative anticipation was correct. I've arranged the vicious cycle in a flowchart.

Negative Assumption Flowchart

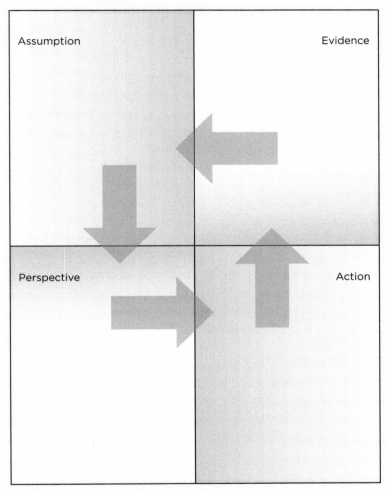

Quadrant one: **Assumption.** For example, say you are invited to a party and your assumption is "The party is going to suck." That flows into . . .

Quadrant two: **Perspective.** If you think the party is going to suck, your perspective will be one of dread or disgust. You're already feeling disappointed and regretful about going. That attitude flows into . . .

Quadrant three: **Action.** Considering your state of mind, you won't bother dressing up for the party, bringing a gift for the host, or making sure your friends will be there. Since you are under-dressed, empty-handed, and don't know anyone, you won't want to talk to anyone and no one talks to you. You will stay for only a few minutes and hate every one of them, flowing into . . .

Quadrant four: **Evidence.** You went, you saw, you confirmed your assumptions, had a bad experience, and came out with con-firmation that parties suck, which reinforces your assumptions, taking you right back into Quadrant one.

Post-insight, you create reality without assumption. If you erased negative assumptions, this entire flowchart would be blank. In any given situation, if you have zero expectations, you could experience countless possible outcomes. Control mastery theory tells us to be wary of any and all anticipatory ideas. They will shape your sense of self and experiences in life.

So much of any outcome is predetermined by how you think and speak about yourself and events. As you create a new nar-rative, rephrase your expectations to shift your perspective away from prophecy and toward reality. The reality is you don't know what is going to happen, but you can strive to have a positive experience. One sure way to do that is to remind yourself **"Life is a mystery that I'm excited to watch unfold. With clear eyes and good intentions, I will do what I can to make things go well."**

With your new identity and narrative, you can create a self-perpetuating cycle of success, of setting positive intentions, pre-paring for good things to happen, judging experiences objectively, and evaluating them to make adjustments and improvements. I've arranged the virtuous cycle in another flowchart.

Positive Intention Flowchart

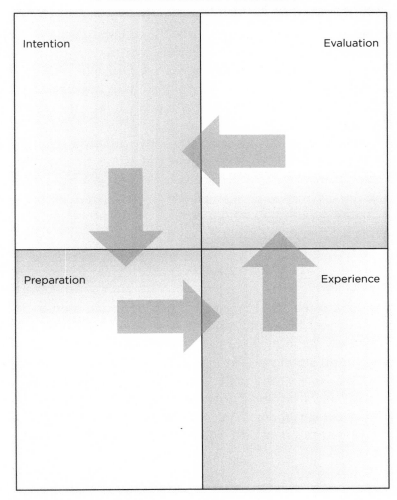

Quadrant one: **Intention.** You are invited to a party and you set the positive intention, "I intend to talk to people, have a good time, and be a gracious guest." That attitude flows into . . .

Quadrant two: **Preparation.** Since you know what you hope to happen, you take action to nudge the outcome in the right direction. You dress well and bring a gift for the host, confirm that other people you know are going, or invite a friend to join you. You think of a few things to talk about with the people you'll meet. That flows into . . .

Quadrant three: **Experience.** You are at the party, making good impressions with your style and conversation. If you start to feel like you've run out of things to say or people to meet, you can always leave early. The point isn't to have the greatest time of your life, but to be present and appreciate it for what it is. This flows into . . .

Quadrant four: **Evaluation.** Was there anything you could have done to have a better experience? Did you set the right intentions and prepare well? Look back on the entire cycle from a third-person POV. The next time you're invited to a party, use all this information to flow into even more focused intentions about how to make it a positive experience.

The Sharp Focus: I present these opposing flowcharts to show you how important it is to think positively, and objectively, about what's actually happening in your reality. Add setting positive intentions to your list of yearly, monthly, weekly, and daily goals. Apply the positivity flow to anything, from what to order in a restaurant to having difficult conversations. When you have a clear progression to follow, you can make strong choices easily and, eventually, automatically.

Have a Life in Full

I've been using the word *positive* a lot. In the domain of positive psychology (see page 234), you can actually measure and coach happiness. One of the leaders of the movement is Martin Seligman, a psychologist, a professor at the University of Pennsylvania, and the author of several best-selling books about human strengths. In *Flourish,* he introduced the acronym PERMA (*positive emotions, engagement, relationships, meaning,* and *achievement*) for the five components of happiness. He and other positive psychology experts have also categorized three types of happy lives:

1. **The pleasant life.** A limited, superficial experience of pleasure and raw positive emotions.

2. **The good life.** Defined by engagement in work and relationships. You know what you're good at and how you can feel fulfilled.

3. **The meaningful life.** A life of giving back and using innate strengths to belong and be of service to something bigger than yourself.

A *full life*, a combination of pleasure, engagement, and meaning, is the happiness trifecta. An *empty life* might have a lot of pleasures but not a lot of engagement or meaning.

In pre-insight days, it might have seemed like a full life was beyond your reach. But now, you are present and conscious, aware of your strengths, and insightful about triggers that might zoom you back to the vulnerability of childhood. You know so much more about your past. You're living mindfully in the reality of the present and bravely taking the leap of faith to live a different way than you always have. A full life of being engaged in the world, contributing to it, and treating yourself to simple (mostly healthy) pleasures is possible. It's the only narrative worth reaching for throughout the rest of your life.

At present, you are very much engaged in the Insight Cure. The deeper your involvement with it, the more you will apply your virtues and strengths and be capable of bringing meaning (or the "boon") to your family, friends, and the whole world.

CREATING A NEW NARRATIVE

Leo

When Leo was getting a handle on his false truth of being unacknowledged and unappreciated, he decided to take positive action to lessen his symptoms and become more engaged. He'd always been an intense runner, and he thought that playing a team sport like basketball would be a socializing alternative. But there was a risk. If he had a rage episode on the court, he'd ruin his new friendships. He decided it would be a good test of his new conscious emotional control.

Leo reported that he'd made a particular friendship with the captain of the team, a man named Luis who, like Leo, was Latino and gay. "This guy never gets ruffled," said Leo in amazement. "Even if he's fouled or catches an elbow. He shrugs it off. I want to be like Luis!"

I encourage all of my patients to look for role models, whether people in their lives or public figures who demonstrate the strengths and qualities they respect, admire, and want to emulate. This is so important! Inspirational people not only show you how it's done, but they are also living proof that your goals can be reached and your problems can be fixed. Remember to pick out someone who "has what you want" as they advise in 12-step recovery, but not someone whose accomplishments and expertise seem so over the top as to be completely out of reach. Also remember to pick someone who is relatable.

Leo's choice—a man he could relate to on many levels—seemed excellent. As the two men got to know each other, Leo and Luis developed a close friendship that reminded me of Campbell's stage when the hero meets a mentor figure (think Obi-Wan Kenobi) as he enters the unknown extraordinary world. Not only had Leo joined a team and made a friend, he'd made advances in several PERMA categories, which soothed him and quieted his inner rage. Plus, he met someone who gave him the acknowledgment and approval he still longed for, even if he'd learned how to deal in its absence. His story shows how "testing" can work.

NARRATIVE TOOL:

Visualization

As you hone and create your identity and new narrative, being able to picture yourself moving through this new life actually helps it become your reality. As you use imagery as a tool, be aware that there is a huge difference between *fantasizing* and *visualizing*. It's like the saying "If you write it down, it's a plan; if you don't, it's a wish."

Fantasizing is the activity of imagining scenarios that satisfy your desire for gratification and vengeance. Fantasizing is wishing, which is not a bad place to start. Fantasy often uses a third-person POV, like watching yourself in the best movie ever, starring you. It might be fun to fantasize, but as a psychological tool that enables you to get what you want in life, it's more or less useless. Fantasy is usually about outcome. You imagine yourself being respected or thin, in a sexual or romantic relationship, or on the beach, but you are no closer to realizing those dreams than you were before you fantasized about them.

Visualizing is like writing it down to make a plan; more specifically, it is making a model in your mind of the process leading to the desired result. Visualizing is a scientific methodology for rehearsing different reality-based scenarios in your head before an important event or interaction. If you learn to visualize effectively, you can condition yourself to succeed, even in stressful, anxious situations.

To visualize for success:

1. First, use the third-person POV to see yourself showing up as required in your life, on task, and with the performance you desire.

2. Next, use the first-person POV, where you enter into the scene and you see and feel the experience. Go over the specifics of a job interview and see yourself being assertive. Feel your steady heart rate. Smell the

confidence. Train your brain to associate walking into that interview with assurance and calm.

3. Visualize every sensation and step. The coldness of the doorknob, the plush carpet under your shoes, the overhead lighting, the sound of the copy machine down the hall. Immerse yourself in detail.

4. Script the scene with positive, powerful phrases, like *I can* and *I am*. I can get the job done. I am the person you're looking for.

5. Repeat the scenario. During the week before the specific event or interaction is to take place, practice daily. Later on, when it's all over, examine how close your visualization was to reality. Even if the two look completely different, you'll be glad you did all you could to be prepared and to succeed.

This is a tried-and-true method of practicing for success. Athletic coaches on the sports field and personal life coaches advocate and outright require this kind of thorough mental preparation. There is no substitute except to rely on luck, which is not really a plan. Prepare, prepare, prepare, and remember what Louis Pasteur said: "Chance seems to favor the prepared mind."

Gut Check

While developing a new narrative, you might feel:

Excited, expectant, or hopeful. You're embarking on a fantastic journey. Of course you should feel optimistic. But you might also feel . . .

Tentative, uncertain, silly, naked, or afraid. The flip side of excitement is nervousness. Don't give in to these emotions. Keep going. It's normal when you are doing something new to worry about whether you really have what it takes to succeed. If you are still insecure, use this reframing technique: Tell yourself you are *excited* rather than just plain old nervous. If you feel the butterflies in your stomach, tell yourself that you are *not* nervous, but *excited*. Of course you are excited about proceeding with your new narrative. It's what you've been working toward all along.

Determined. Good. Always remember the journey that you are on. Widen the lens of your experience and take more into account than you may be feeling in the moment. As the saying goes, if you don't like what you are seeing, draw a bigger circle around it. Take into account all you have done already and get grounded in the here and now, where you actually are. You *are* ready to proceed with your new narrative and revel in your self-efficacy. Take a few deep breaths and meditate on that. Then zoom back in and return to your detailed visualization practice. In this way, you can proceed with your intentions.

PART III

TRANSFORM YOUR LIFE

By constructing a new narrative and putting
it into action, a whole new idea of how your life
can play out becomes imaginable and achievable.

TESTING THE NEW STORY

When you began this journey, you were powerless to disobey the directives of your unconscious mind. You might not even have been aware that it existed, or you might have refused to believe that it was affecting your thoughts and behavior.

Like an explorer, you ventured into the unconscious mind and made important discoveries about your past and how your sense of self and assumptions about life took shape. After reflection, you traced the recurring theme of your false truth throughout your life, changing your outlook forever. Insight is *on*. You've flipped that switch, and you can't go all the way back to blissful ignorance, even if you wanted to.

With faith and bravery, you've worked through life events in the light of your new understanding, and now, with relief and joy (and perhaps a little grief), you've separated yourself from the misconceptions of the past and built a new story about yourself that's based in reality and focused on strength.

You have everything you need to start a new life.

You know where you've been. You know who you are. Now you can move forward with your eyes wide open, expectantly and positively.

One problem: Where do you go from here? There's no sign on the other side that says, "New life, left, 1,000 feet."

The fact is you can go in any direction from here. With all your new knowledge and empowerment, you can venture into the extraordinary, bright, insightful world. All those options can make people feel a bit shaky.

In this chapter, you will test your footing and get a lay of the land. Just like Campbell's mythological heroes, you'll gain confidence via a series of challenges that give you even more insight and control. Each test will put more distance between your childhood misconceptions and your adult reality.

Testing is a huge part of the process of solidifying your new sense of self. You either "pass" a test by using what you've learned, reconfirming the new narrative and keeping your eyes on your goals, or you "fail" by slipping back into false-truth habits and patterns.

It's okay to fail, as long as you understand that you did and why you did. Failing is learning, so in this process, it's a net positive. Don't worry about it! Be glad for the insight, and retest.

Some of the tests will be intentional; others will be accidental. Some will be obvious; others will be subtle. You will learn what constitutes a test and how to assess yourself. Your new identity might take a few hits as you get into the swing of testing, but as you rack up passing grades, you'll become more confident in your strengths. Before long, you won't even need to ask, "Is this a test? How should I react and handle it to pass?" You'll ace tests automatically. Success will be your new pattern.

Testing in a Safe Space

In control mastery theory, therapeutic "testing" is between the patient and the doctor, with "pass" and "fail" grading on both sides of the desk. The patient tests the doctor to establish that it's safe to open up with him. The doctor guides the patient to pass tests with the goal of healing and disproving the patient's false truth.

It's a fascinating part-conscious, part-unconscious process that I'll share with you, and then I'll show you how you've already been "testing" the false truth throughout your life without realizing it. Pre-insight, people tend to fail most of the time by confirming their false truths. Post-insight, with practice and early success, people pass most of the time, disconfirming the false truth and affirming the new narrative.

The two types of testing between a patient and a therapist are **transference** and **passive-into-active**.

TRANSFERENCE

Transference occurs when a patient, acting like a child again and re-creating the same conditions that led to the formation of her pathogenic belief in the first place, transfers these expectations onto the therapist. The patient experiences the therapist like so many other figures from the past. For example, the doctor is commonly put in the role of the parent. An experienced doctor senses this, and thus a patient's test, from a mile away. The patient is by definition completely or all but completely unaware of what she's doing when she initiates the test.

If the doctor reacts in the same way as the patient's actual parent, the patient's false truth is confirmed, which is a major fail for the doctor, since the goal of therapy is to dislodge the pathogenic belief that has been holding the patient back.

If the doctor reacts differently than the parent, the patient's false truth is *not* confirmed. Her unconscious thinks, "Wait a second. There's another way for someone to react to me? Maybe my parents' treatment and my interpretation of what it meant aren't valid." It's like knocking a brick out of the wall of the false truth. By doing so, the doctor passes the test and helps the patient.

Examples of transference testing follow:

1. A patient who believes he was responsible for his
    mother's acute anxiety by being "bad" will test
    the therapist with bad behavior (being disruptive,
    hostile, rejecting, dismissive). If the doctor shows
    anxiety and blames the patient for upsetting her,
    the patient's false truth ("It's all my fault; I make
    people miserable") is confirmed and the doctor fails
    the test and her patient. If the therapist is calm and
    supportive despite the patient's bad behavior, the
    patient's pathogenic belief is challenged. He sees
    that someone isn't sent into a tailspin when he acts
    up. He'll think, "Maybe my mother's acute anxiety
    wasn't my fault." The doctor passes the test and helps
    the patient.

2. A patient whose authoritarian father always told her
    what to do and provoked the child's false truth, "I
    can't be trusted to make my own decisions," might
    repeatedly ask the doctor, "What should I do?" A
    therapist who heaps on advice, lecture style, will fail
    the test by acting like the authoritarian father and
    validating the patient's belief that she can't make
    up her own mind. If the doctor says, "I'm interested
    to know what you think you should do," he passes
    the test, invalidating the patient's false truth and
    providing a safe place for the patient to experience
    decision-making.

The pace and intensity of a patient's tests might seem random and sporadic, but it's all part of an unconscious "plan." The
patient's unconscious mind has a clear agenda, and tests bubble
up and present themselves as needed. He might be completely in
the dark about what's happening (although it might occur to him
that he treats the therapist differently than anyone else). Having
been tested by patients for decades, I can say that it's truly amazing how people play out the same scripts over and over again in
life—and in my office. In the therapeutic process, it's not enough
to pass 1 or 10 tests to dismantle the wall. On average, it takes 20

tests before the patient becomes conscious of the fact that he's testing at all, and then another 20 in therapy and the real world, while working through, to turn the false-truth wall into rubble.

The Sharp Focus: I know it can be confusing. A pass is when you disconfirm. A fail is when you confirm. It seems counterintuitive. But the entire point of therapy is for the patient to break through the wall of misconception-founded assumptions and expectations that have blocked her from realizing her potential. Destruction is good. Destruction is aces. Leaving that wall in place or piling more bricks on top is the opposite of helping someone move forward.

TRANSFERENCE TESTING

Daria

When Daria was a child, she felt like she couldn't reach her parents and that they didn't respond to her when she asked for attention and understanding. They were fairly uptight blue-bloods with a sense of purpose in society—"a fiduciary responsibility," her father would say—who often delegated caretaking to their high-quality staff. It wasn't their style to be unconditionally available, affectionate, or emotional, and neither her mom nor her dad knew how to handle their needy, sensitive daughter. If she cried or reached out, they became flustered and dismissive, often sending her off with a nanny or to her room to be alone, the very opposite of what she was asking for.

A few months into her therapy, Daria transference tested me when she began calling my cell phone repeatedly, sometimes 10 times a day, and sending me videos of her threatening to harm herself if I didn't call her back immediately.

To pass the test and disconfirm her false truth that she'd always be rebuffed by people she tried to connect with, I had to respond differently than her parents. So when she called me, I answered or called her back as soon as possible, and we discussed what she was experiencing for several minutes until she felt better. With repeated reassurances that I was there for her and listening to her, she trusted that I wouldn't disappoint her, and the frequency and intensity of her calls and videos diminished and eventually stopped. When her needs were met, she became less needy. This was a huge revelation to Daria and it will be a huge revelation to you too.

Having very basic needs met creates comfort and allows for maturation. When you get an important need met, you become less needy. In therapy, we discussed transference, and she could see how her unconscious was in effect dialing the phone for her. This insight gave her a degree of control over the urge.

If I had ignored her calls or given her a cold lecture on appropriate behavior and boundaries, I would have failed the test and confirmed her pathogenic belief that no one wanted to "deal with her," as she used to say.

She still has flare-ups sometimes. Consciousness alone isn't a cure. Even if you've been living with a new narrative for a while, there will be times when the false truth and the old story rear their ugly heads. Put into motion a conscious plan to recognize them when they crop up. It'll make all the difference—instead of feeling crushed, then spinning out of control, you'll register a disappointment, and then regain control and master your behavior.

PASSIVE-INTO-ACTIVE

The other type of testing in control mastery theory is the mirror image of transference. It's called *turning passive into active*. In this scenario, the patient unconsciously re-creates the childhood trauma in the therapist's office, but this time, she assumes the active role of her parent and puts the doctor in the passive role of the patient as a child. The tables are turned.

If the therapist reacts the same way the patient did as a child, the patient gets the message, "I was right to feel traumatized and develop a self-defeating narrative and negative assumptions about myself and life." Needless to say, this would be a fail.

If the therapist reacts differently than the child did, the patient would think, "Huh? I treated him badly, and he didn't react like I did. Maybe I can be more like him and react with strength instead of crumbling like a cracker." And that would be a pass.

Passive-into-active testing models for the patient an alternative way to behave that, with encouragement, she can emulate outside the office.

Examples of passive-into-active testing include:

1. A patient whose mother routinely broke promises and withheld attention and gifts develops the false truth "I'm always cheated," and creates the narrative, "I don't deserve to be treated fairly so I expect little from people." In therapy, she takes on the active role of the untrustworthy mother by promising to pay her doctor's bills and then refusing, telling the therapist that he doesn't deserve payment and that he's selfish and greedy to expect anything. If the therapist responds by letting the patient off the hook, somehow justifying her behavior, he fails the test. By tolerating the patient's abuse with affable, depersonalized insistence that he, like everyone, deserves respect and fair treatment, he passes the test and models confidence and self-respect.

2. A patient whose parents were chronically unhappy in their work and miserable in their marriage develops the false truth "Happiness isn't possible" and the old story, "I can't allow myself to be happy in work or love or it'll be a betrayal of my parents." In therapy, he acts like his depressed and defeated parents, insisting that he can't get ahead and is constantly rejected by potential romantic partners. To pass the test, the therapist has to appear enthusiastic and excited about life's possibilities, modeling optimism. If the therapist mirrored the patient's depressing attitude, it would be a big fail.[14]

The Sharp Focus: Whenever I hear people say "I sound just like my mother" or "I'm turning into my father" in casual conversation, I wonder if some aspect of passive-into-active testing is going on. In therapy, it's all too clear when a patient starts behaving like the traumatizing parent, and it's usually with a degree of intensity that would be intolerable in real life. An extreme test—for example, a patient with a verbally abusive father once yelled at me with so much rage, he popped a blood vessel on his nose—indicates just how motivated the patient is to free themselves from the bounds of the false truth.

Testing in the Real World

People test unconsciously all the time, just as they unconsciously befriend and partner with people who confirm what they have always believed to be true about themselves (but isn't). Although you might not realize you're testing, you will definitely feel the pain, however comforting in its familiarity, of replaying the same script over and over again.

I have a patient named Amy whose mother was obsessed (and I don't use that word lightly) with her daughter's weight. The mother cried if Amy gained a pound, and she put Amy on diets from age eight, begged her not to eat, punished her for sneaking treats, harassed her daily, and told her, "Your weight is why I'm unhappy." Amy developed the false truth "My body is shameful; I'm worthless; I cause pain to others by sustaining myself" and the old story that allowed her to salvage a shred of dignity: "It's best to bury my feelings when criticized or rebel hard by doing the opposite of what authority figures tell me to do."

Amy came to see me when her binge eating got out of control. We discussed her dominant emotions of shame, guilt, and anger, a toxic cocktail that had been stewing since she was a little girl.

"One time when I was complaining about my weight to my husband, he said, 'So go on a diet.' I was hurt and angry, but I said nothing. Within a month, I gained ten pounds," she said.

Unconsciously, she'd transference tested her husband. If he'd reacted to her weight gain with anger, tears, and accusations, it would have confirmed Amy's false truth and he would have failed her test.

"How did he react?" I asked.

"He didn't care," she told me. "He said he used the word *diet* because I did, and he was just being supportive. He said he loves me no matter what size I am." Her husband passed the test.

I explained the concept of transference and how Amy re-created her childhood experience by putting her husband in the role of her mother. She worked it through and came back at her next session with a bit of insight. "I realized that every conflict I've had with a boss or a friend was when I felt the tiniest twinge of shame. When my mother shamed me, I crawled into an emotional hole. So if a boss or friend challenged me, I would shut down until I exploded with anger from the pressure of burying my emotions. I've cut people out of my life and been fired a few times for replaying this pattern."

When her husband passed the test, Amy realized that in his eyes, she wasn't shameful, worthless, or a cause of pain. This one test was a big step for Amy to see an alternative life where she didn't have to bury her feelings, sever connections, or feel immense shame about little comments or criticisms.

Experiencing a New Reality

So far, I've given you examples of unconscious testing. Insight is all about consciousness and being present. Part of this process is testing mindfully and intentionally. You'll plan and execute tests that will confirm your strengths multiple times per day. As the romantic poet John Keats said, "Nothing ever becomes real till it is experienced." By testing yourself, you create opportunities to make the new narrative become real. By experiencing life minus the false truth, you free yourself of it.

Look at it this way: You can read about Bali. You can watch videos of Bali. You can dream about it and visualize yourself there. But until you go to Bali and experience the sights, tastes, smells, and sounds for yourself, you have not really experienced it. Bali remains a fantasy realm, even though you know it's real.

By mindfully, intentionally testing your new narrative, you are going to Bali! (Figuratively!) Welcome to an extraordinary world, aka your new life.

MAKE A PLAN

According to control mastery theory, people operate under an unconscious plan. In the Insight Cure, you'll make a conscious plan with two goals:

Prove the old story wrong. As you've being doing for a while, continue to work on bashing expectations and trashing the false truth. Whenever you feel a negative or defeatist assumption coming on, strive to prove it wrong and do whatever you can to experience a different outcome than the one you've previously anticipated.

Prove the new narrative right. Your new narrative is based on personal powers. Jump on any opportunity to use your strengths and virtues (which you circled on pages 157 and 158). Flex your social, mental, and emotional muscles to prove to yourself that your strengths are real and reliable.

Keep a clear focus on your testing plan to accelerate your transformation. Mark your progress on the Experiencing Scale (pages 105–106) and the Changing Scale (page 146). Your ultimate goal is to continually experience your new narrative until it becomes instinct.

ACCUMULATE EXPERIENCES WITH THE NEW NARRATIVE TO REINFORCE IT.

Testing might feel awkward at first, but over time it'll feel more and more natural, until confidence is your new normal.

"Normal" doesn't sound very glamorous, but after decades of negative assumptions and self-sabotage, a life of positivity and strength as a matter of course will make you feel like Superman or Wonder Woman (costume optional).

PREPARE BEFORE TESTING

Plan your testing opportunities, and prepare for them. Don't rush in, as fools do. Impulsiveness is not a strength on Seligman's list, or any other.

Prepare practically. Just as you would prepare for a trip by booking your hotel and plane travel, researching excursions and sights, and packing a suitcase, do the due diligence before a new-narrative test. If you've decided to confirm your strength of social intelligence by going to a networking conference, prepare by RSVPing to interesting panels, Googling the speakers so you can approach them with smart questions, and looking into nearby restaurants so you can invite a new contact out to dinner. It might sound obvious, but if you have the false truth "It doesn't matter what I do" or "No one listens to me," it's possible you've manifested failure by not preparing for success. Reflect on it and remind yourself that you are unlocked from and unblocked by old ideas as you live out new ones.

Prepare mentally. Use insight tools to prepare mentally: Spend five minutes each night on visualization (page 171) by repeatedly rehearsing the test in your mind. Run through the positive intention flowchart (page 167) to help make the necessary mental shift away from negative assumptions. Psych yourself up by using the power phrases *I always*, *I can*, and *I am* about your strengths.

Prepare emotionally. "Why put myself in a situation that might be challenging or stressful? Why force myself to think about my life in a different way or to experience an unfamiliar and possibly uncomfortable reality?" Patients ask me these questions all the time. I always give them the same answer: "You have a duty to yourself to realize your full potential. You have a duty to society to contribute as best you can." It's not just that you deserve to be happy and successful and have a better life than the one you have now. It's that as members of a society, we owe it to others to lift ourselves up. Transcend temporary stress and awkwardness by knowing that it's part of transformation. You're in this for the long run: the rest of a long, happy, healthy life.

Take cues from role models. Watch people who are successful at what you're about to test yourself doing. Notice how they use their strengths of graciousness, kindness, humor, fairness, forgiveness, and open-mindedness to stay positive. If you appreciate their abilities and try to emulate them, you also get the side benefit of erasing negative emotions like jealousy and envy. With one act of switching your perspective from resentment to appreciation, you strengthen yourself.

BEGIN TESTING

As you begin testing, it helps to:

Guarantee early success. The fact is, you don't know what's going to happen when you execute a test—and that's okay. This is a test within a test: how will you handle it when things don't go as you've rehearsed? Surprises give you a fantastic opportunity to test the strength of perseverance and vitality and the insight skills of depersonalizing (third-person POV) and empathizing (looking at every situation from all sides).

That said, try to choose tests that are easy to pass. Set the bar super low at first. It's not that you are so weak and insecure that you have to take baby tests, although it doesn't hurt to be gentle with your new narrative in its infancy. Guaranteeing success takes advantage of human nature: If you pass with flying colors, you will be more motivated to continue testing and to challenge yourself with increasingly difficult tests.

For example, if you had the false truth "I'm invisible; no one sees me or hears me," a good test to guarantee early success would be to attend a gathering of any kind, go up to a complete stranger, and say hello. The person will look at you and probably say something back. There you go. You were seen. You were heard. And now you can turn around and leave with a sense of accomplishment. Up the ante at the next test by saying, "Hello. How are you?" with eye contact. Done. Go home, feel good, and plan your next test. Before you know it, you'll be having friendly conversations with anyone you meet. Increase the challenges incrementally, and only after unequivocal success.

Keep it conscious. As you test your new story in the real world, check in with yourself to make sure you're conscious of what's happening. Every few minutes, do a mental scan. Are you above the waterline of the mind? Are you aware of how unconscious cues might be controlling you? Are you using your strengths? If you were to step outside your body and watch, what corrections would you make? You are the scientist in the lab of life, so put on your invisible white coat. Maintain an objective perspective while examining what you're experiencing.

Repeat. The instructions on a shampoo bottle say, "Repeat as necessary." Regarding testing, your instructions are that repeating *is* necessary. To fire up the synapses in the brain that make new connections between *strength* and *reality*, you have to activate them over and over again. The brain can change, but only by repetition. It's like muscle memory when you play a sport. If you've hit enough tennis balls, your body will perform automatically whenever you pick up a racket. Your brain isn't a muscle, but it can be trained like one. Before you read this book, your brain was trained by your false truth. Now as you live out of insight, repeating strength- and reality-based choices will diminish destructive connections and blaze new creative ones.

EXPERIENCING TOOL:
Micro-tests

A micro-test is a low-stakes confirmation of your new narrative. Do five micro-tests per day, gradually leveling up, for two weeks. To show you how micro-tests work in the real world, I've provided examples from among the patients you've gotten to know while reading the book.

Larry

Larry's false truth was a combination of "I'll never be good enough" and "It doesn't matter what I do," leading him to have multiple affairs and a poor work ethic that kept him stuck in middle management. He selected a few core strengths for his new narrative—gratitude (he was truly grateful to his wife for her patience and love) and appreciation for excellence, even if it made him jealous. I asked him to micro-test himself five times per day by focusing on these two core strengths in any combination he chose and to acknowledge any positive emotions as they came up.

To be grateful: Every day, at least once, he would say thank you to his wife. It could be during breakfast, after a hello kiss, or apropos of nothing in particular. He had incremental level-ups for this test: Saying thank you while looking into her eyes. Then saying it with eye contact *plus* a sentence about what he's grateful for. Then words, eyes, and elaboration *plus* physical contact like holding hands. Gratitude isn't just lip service. Larry was tasked with reflecting on his gratitude for his wife and their life, allowing the emotions that come with thankfulness to fill his heart (just try to look a loved one in the eye and say thank you without getting misty) and associating those powerful, good feelings with his new outlook on life.

To be appreciative: Larry had long been frustrated that he wasn't a star in his professional life. Leadership and innovation were not his strengths, as much as he wished they were. He did have a talent for recognizing the brilliance in others (this was, among other things, what drew him to his wife). So in his consulting job, his micro-tests of this strength were to be appreciative and supportive of his team by saying, "Great job! Good work!" and to search his heart for positive feelings to associate with this expression. How did it make him feel to appreciate and encourage others rather than feeling jealous and depressed that he wasn't as talented as they were? Over a few days or weeks of expressing appreciation, what changes did he notice in his own work and the effort of those around him? To level-up his appreciation, Larry was instructed to offer to help someone else reach his or her goal, and then to ask a team member to teach him how to improve his own skills.

Carrie

Carrie had made huge strides to banish her old story ("If I show any weakness, life will crush me") in several months of therapy. She'd been forced by chance—a bad car accident that left her immobile and dependent on friends and family—to confront the validity of her false truth. She realized that by allowing herself to show vulnerability, she strengthened herself and her relationships. The feeling of connection she had in the aftermath of the car accident would be just another temporary exceptional experience, however, if she couldn't repeat it. Carrie had many strengths to test—creativity, fairness, kindness, curiosity, and integrity. I was concerned that fear of expressing negative emotions could hamper her early success, and I tailored her micro-tests to be positive and fun.

To be creative: Her creativity in art and music had always been a source of comfort and joy for her. But when she was paralyzed by a life challenge, she avoided her sketch pad and guitar. Her micro-test was to draw or play every day, regardless of whether she was inspired or in the mood. Afterward, she was tasked with exploring how it felt to be in control of her creativity and to judge her work with a third-person POV. Was the sketch any good? How could it be better? Level-ups for this test were spending more time on creativity, not only judging her work but striving to improve it, and then sharing her work with friends or online.

To be curious: Carrie had a tendency to hole up in her apartment when life got too hard. Solitude and safety comforted her, but they also played into the false truth that she was incapable of handling stress. Her micro-test was to go on a mission outside her apartment every day, letting her strength of curiosity and love of learning be her guide. What restaurant made the best cheeseburger in town? How many of her neighbors had interesting landscaping? She would reflect on the positive emotions of being out and about and on how minor negative emotions (irritation about missing the bus, etc.) couldn't undo her. This micro-test would confirm that it was safe and fun to explore her world and emotions. To level up, Carrie could go on quests that were farther afield, in new places and events she hadn't been exposed to before.

FAILING A MICRO-TEST

Claudia

Claudia was a wonderful, generous, highly competent woman, a gifted musician with an amazing sense of direction. She almost never got lost. And yet she felt hopeless about her life. She did a lot for other people and couldn't help wondering if anyone would ever take care of her as well as she did of them. In therapy, we sorted out her false truth—that she expected adult friendships and relationships to be equal to the unconditional devotion and adoration her mother showed her. If a relationship wasn't defined by selflessness and sacrifice, it didn't seem real or worthy to her.

In our sessions, Claudia worked through how her too-high expectations and dashed hopes affected her. As she identified her strengths—honesty, vitality, bravery, and perseverance—Claudia realized they all fell under the virtue category of courage. Her new narrative was "Zesty woman bravely sticks to her guns and toughs things out." Her new narrative sounded a lot like her old one—with a critical difference. She was no longer gunning to do her absolute best at all times. We discussed the benefit of rounding out her new narrative by developing other strengths, specifically those under the virtue of transcendence, such as faith, gratitude, and appreciation. If she tested grace and repeatedly passed, it would provide a counterbalance to her grit.

As her birthday rolled around, I suggested she test faith, and ask her sister to throw her a little party. She promised to make it a blast. They set a date, and she told Claudia all she'd have to do was show up. Claudia was filled with discomfort at handing her the reins. It triggered her false-truth belief that if she didn't go above and beyond for her, it would prove she didn't really love her. "I'm not testing her love," she reminded herself in our sessions. "I'm testing my own ability to be grateful for any effort she makes, to appreciate her for who she is, and to have faith that she loves me, even if this party sucks, which I'm sure it will."

As the date drew near, Claudia's anxiety grew. She had to bite her tongue not to ask her about the food and RSVPs. We discussed the real source of her anxiety, which was the fear that she'd blow it and let her down, making her feel hopeless and alone. The pressure proved too much. The day of the party, a backyard barbeque, Claudia arrived two hours early to her sister's house to inspect the preparations. Claudia wound up taking over her own party, feeling resentful that her sister hadn't been more involved. She had hired a local restaurant to supply the food and had her husband prepare some decorations. She resented her lack of special attention and apparent thoughtlessness and lack of consideration. Her sister resented Claudia's lack of appreciation. The party was a letdown, just as she'd expected.

If Claudia had focused on her positive intention of receiving love in any form, she may have been able to realize that perhaps her sister's generic party was actually the best she could muster—*her* best as distinct from *Claudia's* best. It was really all about expectation management and learning to expect what others had to offer. Instead, she doubled down on her false truth and on this occasion proved herself right, failed the test, and had a pretty terrible time.

EXPERIENCING TOOL:

Macro-tests

It might take a couple of weeks to pass your micro-tests consistently. The act of testing alone is a success, so don't concern yourself with perfection. Just keep at it, and after a while you will start to pass with consistency. After passing a micro-test five times a day for two weeks, with gradually increasing degrees of difficulty, you're ready to move on to macro-tests.

Macro-tests, as the name implies, are larger in scope. A micro-test would be speaking to one person at a meeting; a macro-test would be addressing a whole room of people, perhaps as a panelist or as the host of an event. Macro-tests mark exponential growth, but they're really just an expanded version of tests that you have already passed.

Continue testing and passing three micro-tests every day *as well as* executing one macro-test per week for three weeks. Mark the macro-tests on your calendar. Prepare for them as best you can with daily deadlines. And then show up for the test, stay mindful, and be open to any outcome. With each pass, you will confirm your new narrative and forge brain connections that link experience with an instinct for success. As you test yourself, remember to

1. confirm the new narrative;

2. forge brain connections that link experience with an instinct for success;

3. use your strengths;

4. step outside yourself to view the interaction with a third-person POV;

5. see it from all sides, in 3-D;

6. have no expectations, only good intentions;

7. be mindful of intense emotions and how they might relate to your false truth; and

8. forgive yourself for momentary slips into the old story, and then shift back to the new narrative.

As with the micro-tests, I'll provide some examples from the macro-tests of some of my patients.

Bobby

Bobby's strengths were love, kindness, hope, forgiveness, and fairness, all of the things he blindly gave away to the so-called friends who lied to him and took advantage of his generosity. For his micro-tests, Bobby worked on bestowing all those altruistic strengths *on himself.* He was to show himself love and forgiveness every day, in whatever way he could, by treating himself with kindness and replacing self-criticism with fairness. It was a tall order to ask a man who had given so much of himself to others to give to himself, but after several weeks of micro-testing, Bobby understood the importance of valuing himself so that he was better able to judge the value in others.

As he progressed to macro-testing, Bobby was presented with a golden opportunity. One of his abusive brothers was getting married back home, and Bobby was required to attend the wedding. Going home, family weddings, holidays, high school and college reunions, and funerals are macro-tests we all have to face, and they're not easy! One of my very best supervisors in San Francisco was a brilliant psychiatrist named Steve Purcell. I spent years with him as my supervisor and mentor and continue to regard him as a gifted, suave, subtle, crafty, and naturally intelligent guy. One day, he was explaining why we wouldn't be meeting for the next two weeks, and he started complaining about having to go home to see his family in Georgia. I said, "But Dr. Purcell, how can this be a problem for *you*?" A man of his knowledge and confidence was rattled by going home?

He said, "It's like falling off a log."

He meant that it was only too easy to revert to old behaviors. That stuck with me. No matter how well you prepare, being in the old environment with the people who installed the false truth into your brain in the first place is the granddaddy of macro-tests. People treat you the same way, and you feel as awkward and ill-equipped as you used to. All of the old hurts, insecurities, and patterns come roaring back. The phrase *back home* is so apt. Emotionally, you go backward.

For Bobby to pass his macro-test, he had to bring all of his strengths to the wedding with him. Growing up, his brothers teased and beat him mercilessly. His father laughed along at the "horseplay," and his mother didn't protect him. Bobby soothed himself with the narrative "I don't fit in here, but when I find people I relate to, everything will be great!" While working through the old story, he had to pull off his too-trusting blinders and learn to make reality-based judgments about people. To internalize his new narrative, he had to put his own feelings first and treat himself with the same loving generosity and forgiveness he'd given to others.

"Usually, when I go home, my brothers punch me in the arm or put me in a headlock. I feel helpless and humiliated, and I have to laugh along or lose face. I can't believe I put up with it for so long," he told me.

Bobby used visualization to rehearse a different reaction. "I rehearsed blocking the punches and twisting out of the headlock. But I realized it was one thing to visualize the ninja moves and another to actually do them. So I signed up for a self-defense class."

He was taking on a new challenge and experiencing himself in a different way. Bobby was so prepared to face his brothers' violence that he couldn't wait to go home again. As it turned out, his older brother was on good behavior in front of the bride's family and never got physical with Bobby, nor did his other brother. "I was so disappointed! But on the other hand, the cake was delicious," he said, laughing. Needless to say, Bobby passed the test.

Leo

For Leo to live out his new narrative, he had to tamp down his rage episodes. We discussed what strength he could use to control his anger, and he suggested humility. He'd had a humble background. If he could be mindful of how far he'd come and feel proud of himself for it, he wouldn't depend on the praise of others to satisfy his "way to go, Leo" needs.

While working through how his false truth had affected his life, Leo looked closely at his romantic history. "I doomed them all," he said and described episodes of transference testing failures. "I forced every man I ever loved to act like my father and reject me. It wasn't fair to them, and it definitely was my fault."

In addiction recovery therapy (for more info, go to page 229), a healing step is to understand how the addiction affected loved ones and to make amends for your behavior. The wording of Alcoholics Anonymous's step eight is "Make a list of all persons we've harmed, and become willing to make amends to them all." And step nine: "Make direct amends to such people wherever possible, except when to do so would injure them or others." Leo's rages were in a way like binge-drinking episodes, and he had harmed people besides himself. His macro-tests would be to make amends to those people and to practice humility by apologizing to them. "I was wrong, and I'm sorry" is one of the most powerful statements one person can make to another.

Leo planned this test of humility by calling up three ex-boyfriends and making dinner dates with each of them. He prepared by visualizing an evening of clarity and restraint. He had no agenda or expectations about the conversation. He only had the positive intention of saying "I'm sorry" and conveying genuine regret.

Leo and I met in my office a day or two after each dinner. About the first date he said, "It was really awkward. I talked about gaining insight and working through my false truth, and the guy just blinked at me. I didn't go in with expectations, but he sure did, and it was not to sit around and talk about our childhood traumas. He walked out before we even ordered. I felt okay about it though."

His second dinner went better. "I knew to ease into the conversation this time. This guy had been in therapy, and he understood what I was trying to do. He said that sometimes making amends comes off as selfish, and that he felt a bit used by being part of my test. That's when the *real* test started for me. Anger bubbled up, but I stepped outside of myself and saw it from his perspective. He was pissed at me and had been for a long time. He had every right to be, so I just repeated how sorry I was. We left on okay terms. I don't think we'll be friends, but it was progress."

On his third test, Leo was empathetic from the very beginning of the meal. "That was the breakthrough. I was able to make amends by creating the opportunity for him to express his feelings, and man, he had a lot to get off his chest. By the end of the meal, I knew his perspective and exactly what I was apologizing for." He walked out with a whole new attitude about all his interactions, past and future, which is a major pass of his macro-test.

FAILING THE MACRO-TEST

Steve

As Steve and his wife hastened through their divorce proceedings, Steve continued to live out his old story by sugarcoating his problems so they'd magically go away. As he'd done for decades, he used drugs and alcohol to numb himself.

It was a challenge for Steve to identify any strengths in himself. He chose humor and honesty. Since his false truth was to lie to himself about life, I wasn't sure honesty was a good fit. We discussed it and decided to call honesty "realism." His new narrative was, "I used to gloss over painful experiences, but now I see it like it is and will respond respectfully to what's really going on."

He worked through a series of micro-tests that included assessing the reality of his health (by keeping doctors' appointments), his finances (by visiting an accountant), and his addiction (by attending AA meetings). He did it all, but I had my doubts about the depth of his emotional experiences.

An opportunity for a macro-test presented itself when his wife's lawyer called a meeting with Steve to finalize the divorce settlement. "I don't want to lose her, but what can I do?" he asked with uncharacteristic seriousness and vulnerability, which I took as a positive sign. We discussed how he should prepare and behave at the settlement meeting to emphasize his strength of realism. His mission was to react with genuine emotion—no jokes or sugarcoating. If something made him sad, he should be sad. If something made him glad, he should be glad. His wife's longtime main complaint was that he refused to deal with his problems. "Maybe if she sees I'm trying to change, she'll take me back," he said. That was a particularly dangerous expectation, so we discussed going in with positive intentions, realism, and an open heart.

Which he did. At first. When his genuine sadness didn't change his wife's attitude, he reverted to making jokes and acting like he didn't care. If he'd passed the test, the outcome would have been the same, but he would have strengthened his realism for future interactions. Instead, he confirmed his old story and failed.

Steve didn't really have the same goals for himself that I did for him. This made for a big problem in his treatment. I wanted him to realize that "Fake it till you make it"—which can work when you are trying out a new pattern of response to life coupled with self-awareness, emotional connectedness, and a desire to change—was not working and would not work for him. He didn't want to change. He coped by ignoring problems.

Steve was hearing me and was allowing me to influence him, but he wasn't inclined to directly acknowledge that or give me the benefit of knowing that he was changing. But there were encouraging sights. Reports from his family about his easier demeanor and greater sense of presence at family gatherings and on the job (he worked for his brother, who updated me from time to time) were encouraging. He had a healthy routine, was free from alcohol and drugs, began exercising, and was starting to lose some excess weight. I hoped he'd keep it up.

The Power of "Don't Hold Me Back"

As you engage in testing, you'll take a close look at others' behavior too. Testing is not only about you, it's about *them*.

Are your friends, family, or partners passing tests or failing you?

Just as recovering alcoholics should avoid their drinking buddies, you might need to steer clear of people who have a stake in keeping you locked and blocked. Co-dependent people—those who need you to be damaged so they can play out their own false truth—will try to undermine you by discounting your strengths, calling your insight journey "stupid" or "useless," criticizing you ("You were a lot more fun before"), and making veiled threats ("I don't know if I can take this change in you").

You might need to add new people to your life and get rid of some old ones. Many patients of mine have come to realize that their partners were in their lives for one reason: to confirm their false truth. When they tried to live a new narrative, the significant others couldn't tolerate the positive change. In some cases, people had to leave their codependent partners to move forward. Insight is that powerful. It casts a new light on all of your interactions, including your closest relationship. To make real, deep, wholesale changes, you will have to have very sober discussions with those you have intimate relationships with.

Whenever someone dismisses your path or tries to lure you back into false-truth patterns of thinking and behavior, you can stop them with the phrase "Don't hold me back." These four words, spoken in a strong, authentic voice with eye contact, are very powerful. It's not a threat or a warning. It's a serious statement of intention, a message of hope, and an invitation for your partner or friend to come along for the ride with you. Your intimate might react in any number of ways.

> **Positively.** If the person gives you a positive response, as in "I'll support you in whatever you want to do," they might be absolutely sincere. Or they might just be saying what you want to hear. Take it with a grain of salt. The closer someone is to you, the more likely it is that they are in your life to either confirm or disconfirm your false truth. Their immediate reaction might not provide a good clue as to which role they play. Wait and watch consciously as you move forward with your new narrative.

> **Negatively.** If you get a negative response, as in "This is stupid. I don't care what you do. I'm not changing for you, and I want you to stay the same," or anything that gives you the sinking feeling that this person is invested in your staying locked and blocked, be wary. They might come around over time, or they might be an obstacle to your growth. Give them a wide berth, at least for the time being, and go elsewhere to share your progress.

> **Confused.** "What does that mean? How are you changing?" An open-minded person who has some experience with therapy or inner work will be curious and interested. Say, "I had an idea about myself from childhood and it's affected how I behave. But I'm not going to let it control me anymore." The interaction could turn into a valuable

talking through experience for you and a revelatory first step toward insight for your friend. It could strengthen the friendship as you discuss the concepts and align your insight journeys. Or opening up about your inner work could lead to an emotional gap between you. If the person is closed-minded, the gap might widen to such an extent that the relationship can't be sustained. You just don't know and can't (and shouldn't) predict how revealing your journey will affect other people.

The fact is, there are a million ways this conversation could go, and that's fine. You are no longer attached to any particular outcome. You have no negative assumptions, only positive intentions. Saying "Don't hold me back" asserts your strength and commitment to live a different, better life, either with your partner or friend or without.

You can have some sympathy for people who don't get it. They've experienced you and their relationship with you only one way. They might feel insulted, blindsided, or left behind by your intention to move forward regardless of their feelings. A real friend will try to grow alongside you. You can't leave someone behind if she's keeping up. If an important person in your life refuses to try, or worse, undermines your process, he *is* holding you back. You may then really have no other choice but to cut ties with that person.

Often, we gravitate toward or unconsciously select people who serve to reinforce our false truths, and they are unhealthy elements in our lives. Perhaps you can change the nature of your regard for someone and together change the tone of the relationship you share or, more often, perhaps not.

In any relationship, when you have moved past what is there, or when you realize that what is there is actually unhealthy, then you must move on. Ask, "Do I feel energized by my encounters with *x*? Do we share a good energy?" If the answer isn't a firm yes, then it's time to let *x* go. Move away from negative energy and emotion and toward positive energy and emotion whenever possible. Not impulsively, of course, but considerately, respectfully, and carefully.

Gut Check

During this testing step, you might feel:

Awkward. Whenever you have an awkward moment, it is often a slight reversion to your old pattern of behavior. Before you gained insight, the experience would have been devastating. But now that you're changing, it's merely awkward. Whenever you get that "shoot me now" feeling—especially if you can laugh about it—it's a real sign of progress. If you can spend 20 minutes each week reflecting on how and why the situation happened and how it relates to the old narrative, I promise that these awkward moments will decrease rapidly.

Sad. Losing friends who fail your tests might make you sad in the short term. But in the long run, you'll benefit from clearing the emotional space to allow new people and healthy relationships into your life. You are not obligated to maintain false-truth confirming connections.

Shaky. I have observed that when my patients start testing, something is sure to happen that could throw them off their new narrative and zoom them right back to living with their false truth. With vigilance and foresight (the simple act of reading this chapter and preparing for tests and executing them several times per day), you'll be ready to face challenges and grade yourself on how well you get through them. As you accumulate "pass" grades, you'll feel more steady.

Relief. Once bad habits are gone and false-truth confirming friends are ousted, after a bit of sadness, you will feel sweet relief. You are free from unconscious oppression in your own mind and from the people who reinforced the behavior that kept you down. Now you can rush forward into your new world with freedom and enthusiasm. No one is holding you back, including yourself.

MAKING CHANGE STICK

You've just about made it. You've arrived at the last step in the Insight Cure: maintaining and further developing the new narrative until it becomes second nature. Take a moment to appreciate how much you've already accomplished.

You've examined your patterns, linked them to early memories, and unearthed the responses you had to painful experiences from early childhood that shaped your sense of self and how you fit into the world.

You've dragged painful memories to the surface and examined them more closely than you ever have before to gain deeper insight into your false truth and how it has been affecting you for your whole life.

You've worked through the false truth and learned to see it from multiple angles, with objectivity and empathy, alleviating some of the pain it caused.

You have allowed insight to shine from within, through the cracks, to further illuminate the past, and to light a way forward into a new existence of endless possibilities that may be a bit frighteningly, and thrillingly, unfamiliar.

You've started to develop a whole new identity based on your strengths and talents. You've committed to using them to reach your full potential as an individual and to meet your obligation to contribute the best of yourself to the rest of the world.

You've tested your new identity, walking the walk and feeling the feelings, to prove to yourself and to the people in your life that you are not attached to your childhood misconception anymore. You are living as a new person, with positive intentions and confidence.

To get this far, you have done a tremendous amount of heavy emotional lifting. If you've been taking adequate time for each step, three to six months have gone by since you cracked open this book. If you've read ahead to understand the scope of the process before undertaking each step, that's okay too, as long as you reread each chapter as you do the work of it, and give it as much time and attention as you can. We live in a rush-rush 24/7 culture where people expect instant gratification, a quick fix. Who wouldn't want to be instantly cured of depression, anxiety, addictions, and other self-defeating habits and patterns overnight? Who wouldn't want to jettison insecurity like so much garbage into the trash cans outside? But insight doesn't work that way. It takes weeks to heal a skinned knee and months to heal an emotional wound from childhood.

Consciously, you can decide to change, logically understand every step in the process, and expect to hit predictable benchmarks of improvement. Unconsciously, however, your mind isn't going to give up its entrenched beliefs and patterns without a fight. Stumbling, lurching, falling, sliding back, correcting are all part of the process. The path to confidence is more like a corkscrew than a straight line.

As you enter this stage of making the boons of insight stick, be mindful of old patterns and give yourself permission to feel confused at times, a bit shaky, and occasionally doubtful. Every emotion is valid as you explore and experience your new life. If a negative thought or assumption comes up and seems to be related to the false truth, look hard at it as always, and work it through.

This last step—making change stick, or what Prochaska called the maintenance stage of change—might feel like two steps up, one step back. It takes between six and twelve months to cement a new set of assumptions about life and redraw patterns of behavior. You spent years, probably decades, living life a certain way. Several months of transition doesn't seem like too much to ask. As you go, you'll make wholesale positive changes and will ultimately be an expert at navigating a brand-new world. Before you know it, it'll look just as familiar as the old one—but a lot more welcoming.

Success Brings Success

Nothing is quite as encouraging and motivating as success. Every time you reinforce your new narrative, you'll feel more empowered to do it again, to keep the trend line moving in the right direction. It might not always feel like you are changing on a day-to-day or week-to-week basis, and that's actually a good sign.

A good comparison is the pace of weight loss. If you drop 20 pounds in a month due to some extreme, restrictive diet, the change isn't going to stick. You won't be able to maintain the eating plan, will revert to old habits, and will regain the weight, setting off feelings of hopelessness and impotence that make future change unlikely. It's really not too hard to *temporarily* change your habits. But to *permanently* change emotional habits, the ones that put you on a self-defeating cycle to begin with, you will have to go deeper, and that takes time.

OCCASIONAL SETBACKS ARE A CHANCE TO ASSERT THE NEW NARRATIVE.

Pre-insight, a "cheating" episode (to keep the metaphor going) would crush the entire diet (or your outlook on life). Now you can view a minor reversion as a golden opportunity to test your strength and prove to yourself that you aren't crushed by challenges. The hero has to make mistakes so he can learn from them and use that knowledge later on when he faces a major ordeal. If you charted your progress over time, you'd be able to see that the occasional setback is part of a larger pattern of forward momentum.

I believe in regular assessment as a component of progress. Every few weeks, I take the measure of a patient's confidence using six sliding scales. Where does he put himself? Closer to one side or the other? Right in the middle?

Sliding Scales of Confidence

Mood scale

Happiness ——————————|—————————————— Anxiety

Thoughts scale

Realistic thoughts ————————|———————————— Negative thoughts

Behaviors scale

Healthy/Assertive ——————|————————————— Unhealthy/Unwanted

Relationships scale

Harmony ——————————|————————————— Conflict

Life satisfaction scale

High ————————|————————————————— Low

Quality of life scale

Active/Engaged ——————————|————————————— Inactive/Isolated

Once I have a measure of the patient's state of mind, we discuss specific short-term goals. If a patient assesses his quality of life as *inactive/isolated*, he's tasked with exercising and seeing more people during the upcoming week. When he returns to therapy, we discuss whether he met his goal or not. If he did, we'll talk about how it feels to be engaged and active. If he didn't, we'll talk about how the false-truth related excuses kept him from reaching his goal.

From my side of the desk, I also assess a patient's confidence and progress by how I feel in the context of our relationship. As therapy progresses and patients are able to move away from their false truth, I can feel their presence in the room differently. It's less guarded. Distance is replaced by a sense of closeness. Patients change remarkably before my eyes. At first, most are tense and compressed into themselves (legs and arms crossed, back hunched, short breaths). As they gain awareness and insight, their bodies visibly relax. They sit with their arms on the back of the chair, breathing easily, with their torsos open. As comfort and confidence grow, they speak with less formality and rigidity and are increasingly willing to disclose more memories, feelings, and truths. It's not my skill as a doctor that changes their manner and body language. Instead, they are able to open up—body, heart, mind, and soul—over time, as the grip of false truth–related shame, fear, guilt, and insecurity loosens. If I notice a patient tightening up and withholding again, it's often a clue that she's falling back into old-story assumptions and habits.

MAINTENANCE TOOL:

False Truth Log

The aim of Cognitive Behavior Therapy (CBT) (see page 231 for more info) is behavior modification through awareness. It's a practical approach to unlearning bad behaviors and establishing good ones. CBT isn't appropriate for deep inner work, but if you have bad habits to break, it helps. I've seen the benefits of CBT in people with severe insomnia and obsessive-compulsive disorders (OCD). If you are made aware of your emotional state, time of day, location, the people you're with, and other circumstances when you are compelled to do something, like smoke a cigarette or pull out your hair (a fairly common OCD called trichotillomania), then you can manage the impulse in the moment, learn to predict and prepare for it, lessen the intensity of the compulsion, and eventually avoid the behavior altogether.

It's all about turning mindless action into mindful resistance. In a way, your old story—the assumption you had about life that controlled your feelings and actions—was a mindless (or unconscious) habit. If you raise your awareness and make your behavior mindful, you can get control over it and change it. As a mindfulness exercise, try keeping a log of whenever false-truth reactions pop up. What dominant emotion came up? What were you doing at the time? Where were you? With whom? How does the reaction relate to the false truth? How aware were you of it? What was the intensity of it? Did you resist reverting to old-story behavior? How did you feel?

False Truth Log

	Intense Emotion	Place Activity People	How Relates to False Truth	Awareness (1 to 5)	Urge to React Negatively	Resist? Yes or No	Feelings Afterward
Monday							
Tuesday							
Wednesday							
Thursday							
Friday							
Saturday							
Sunday							

Sliding Back

Insight itself will not cure you. The practiced application of insight will allow you to get used to and comfortable with the new reality you have to experience in the world. This is the Insight Cure. The world is not always going to make it easy for you. Life will throw you some curveballs no matter how deeply you've internalized the new narrative, and sometimes your confidence will be rattled.

All those assumptions about life that you detached from will try to reattach and retake control. The false truth does not know how to take a hint and leave you alone. You have to reject it over and over again.

The false truth is persistent and sneaky. It might catch you unawares. Since the old story feels comfortable and familiar, you might perceive regression into it as "right." Your unconscious will send a message to your conscious that your false-truth self is the "real you," and that the new identity is "fake." A common emotion during this stage of the Insight Cure is confusion. What's right? What's real? You thought you knew, and then you weren't 100 percent sure.

As a therapist, I'm trained to look for clues that a patient's unconscious is taking control again. When I hear him or her speak certain phrases, I know it's time to look at what's going on and how the false truth has reasserted itself.

Clue #1: "I knew this was bullshit!"

When a patient says this, he might think he's expressing frustration and doubt about the process. What I hear is false-truth insecurity and inadequacy, as in "I was wrong to believe I could experience myself and life in any other way. I'm a loser and I'll always be a loser." By insisting that change is impossible, the patient is confirming the false truth that he *is* worthless, and *isn't* capable of living a full, happy life.

The "bullshit" remark might lead to a complete abandoning of the new narrative, or it could be the death cry of the false truth.

I always remind my patients that old habits die hard. Your pathogenic belief was how you thought about yourself for a very long time. Before it's completely banished from your mind, it will seize any opportunity to get its hook back into you. The "bullshit" feeling has a dark history. Shine the beam of insight onto the frustration and defeatism you're experiencing. Is this the false truth talking? Then you know not to listen.

I also remind my patients to forgive themselves for their doubt and insecurity. We live in complicated times, and we're all tested by extreme and sudden challenges—an illness, a death, financial trouble, relationship problems. Life does not always run smoothly, and there will be times when you feel overwhelmed. When you were vulnerable and afraid as a child, you reacted a certain way. Know that as an adult, vulnerable, frightening moments are when you'll be most susceptible to false-truth thinking. The difference is that you are not a child anymore. You're an insightful adult with a strength-based identity.

Instead of saying "It's all bullshit," try this instead: **"I'm overwhelmed right now, but I'm still the hero of my own life. I will always face trials and tests. I'll pass some and learn from all of them."**

Clue #2: "I failed a test. The whole thing is ruined!"

As long as you're mindful and engaged, there's no failure in insight. There is only testing, experimenting, and experiencing.

People with "It's all my fault" false truths are afraid that one bad decision or one slip into the old story "ruins" the entire process. The messy truth is that you probably won't pass every test of the new narrative, especially the kind that you can't prepare for.

Perfection is a negative assumption. It's also unrealistic, which makes it anti-insight. One slip doesn't ruin the process. Making mistakes, understanding what happened, and using this knowledge to grow stronger *is* the process!

So instead of letting a slip turn into a downward spiral, the "it's all ruined" patient and I focus on the emotions she's experiencing and reflect on how it relates to the false truth. We talk about alternative reactions and look at her life realistically. And then, after falling off the log, as my friend and mentor Steve Purcell would say, we discuss the best way to regroup and get back on.

Instead of saying "It's ruined!" try this instead: **"I used to feel out of control if things didn't go right. Now I react with understanding and objectivity no matter what happens."**

CLUE #3: "I FEEL SO STRONG, I CAN HANDLE ANYONE OR ANYTHING."

As you work through the false truth and internalize the new narrative, be vigilant about guaranteeing positive outcomes. One way to do that is to avoid risky people and places that zoom you right back in to your old story and destructive habits.

If a patient tells me he's internalized the new narrative so deeply that he's not worried about major life challenges or being surrounded by underminers, I think, "Uh-oh." There is such a thing as too much faith and bravery while making a significant attitudinal shift.

With insight, you have a deep understanding of yourself and how your mind works. This understanding gives you control. Mastery comes from testing and experiencing yourself minus the false truth. Through experience, you confirm your new sense of self and gain confidence.

Confidence is the end result of experience. Over-confidence, on the other hand, is a sign you're still operating by the false truth. Your old story was a deeply embedded addiction. Do not underestimate the power of an addiction. The first tenet of any recovery therapy is to try to avoid people, places, and things that trigger cravings for the abused substance. Thus in overcoming your old story, you try to avoid the people, places, and things that push false-truth buttons. Keep a tight hold on your new sense of yourself, your precious, loving, deserving self. Be like Odysseus, who lashed himself to the mast as he sailed on his voyage so that he would not succumb to the sound of the Sirens bent on seducing him to return to their island and his certain death.

Instead of saying "I got this, no problem," try this instead: **"I'm walking a new path that does not include the same old haunts."** Or you can take a line from Alcoholics Anonymous: **"Nothing changes if nothing changes."** Keep going on your journey and remember that you only have to be concerned with doing "the next right thing."

CLUE #4: "I DID EVERYTHING RIGHT, AND IT'S NOT WORKING."

When someone complains about following the rules and being cheated out of an expected outcome, what I hear is the false truth "I'll never get what I want."

Irvin Yalom wrote that to be a well-adjusted person, you have to accept that life isn't fair. Even after you've worked through the Insight Cure, there's no guarantee that the people you interact with are healthy themselves. Or you could get a healthy person on a bad day. If you're testing the new narrative "People care what I have to say," and you test with an unhealthy person, you might get shut down. But that only proves the other person is rude or obnoxious or any number of things. If someone is horrible to you, it does not mean that you are horrible. It means that she is. As we say in Addiction Recovery Therapy, don't judge your inside against someone else's outside. You have no idea what the other person's false truth is and how it affects his behavior. Your power comes from your insight into who *you* are, as well as from your empathy about whatever someone else might be going through.

Instead of saying "It's not working," try this instead: **"I see the world from a realistic perspective. I will always try to maintain a balanced mind, understand what and why I do and feel things, and control my behavior accordingly."**

CLUE #5: "I SHOULD BE HAPPIER BY NOW."

The word *should* is a giant false-truth red flag. It means you are anticipating a certain outcome. The outcome might be positive (happiness), but even if it were negative (disaster), the end result would be the same. If you anticipate happiness and don't get it, you are less happy than you would have been if you'd expected nothing. You can aspire to contentment and joy, hope for them, and even prepare for them. But *should* makes happiness conditional—requirements must be met or else. *Should* is a setup for disappointment and discouragement. Instead, keep a mentality of reality—what *is*, not what should be. Also, *should* smacks of entitlement. None of us are owed happiness. I believe we all deserve it and are capable of realizing it. I also believe that deep joy comes from contributing your gifts and strengths to the world, which is the opposite of feeling bitter about how the world has failed you.

Instead of saying, "I should feel happy," try this instead: **"I'm open to remaining as present as possible."**

Bouncing Back

Positive psychology and the study of resilience tells us a lot about the importance of pursuing your goals by believing in yourself and in your ability to carry on. This may be one of the most important ideas to hold on to throughout your journey.

Sports teaches us to "never ever ever give up." Life, of course, does too. Persistence is a by-product of undertaking this journey. You have it. You've got this now. What insight takes, more than anything else at this point, is persistence. That means standing up and keeping on going every time after you fall.

It is important to remember that resilience is doable. In my medical training, *doable* was the watchword every day. No matter how tired we were, no matter how daunting something seemed (admitting a patient to the intensive care unit for the first time and writing all the necessary orders or caring for a pediatric patient who didn't understand why she was in the ER), knowing that this—whatever it was—was in fact doable proved sustaining beyond belief.

To complete your journey, you must hold on to those sustaining beliefs.

A Japanese proverb tells us, "Fall seven times; stand up eight." Your capacity to bounce back after a fall is key to growing and incorporating new learning about yourself into your worldview going forward. Your new, healthy, fair, uncompromised set of expectations about yourself in relationship to the world is the result of having recognized and moved away from your false truth and into living with fresh vision. When you stumble, this does not mean all is lost. Take a breath, stay present, right yourself, and then continue on the path.

Reshape Your Brain

Neuroplasticity of the brain means that the brain can change, even in people over 40. New synapses can be developed; old ones can be diminished and eliminated. The way to change your brain is to change your thoughts, and hence, your behavior.

Using fMRI machines, one thing scientists can see is the brain's resting-state connectivity. It's like a 3-D image of how your brain has been wired over a lifetime of experiences. This technology has been useful for doctors to see, say, how the brain of a depressed person is wired differently than a non-depressive. According to my colleague Susan Whitfield-Gabrieli Ph.D., a Principle Research Scientist at the McGovern Institute for Brain Research at MIT, "Recent research has shown that individuals who have experienced childhood trauma of various magnitudes exhibit aberrant resting-state networks."[15] In other words, the unconscious narrative appears in the geography of your brain. "However," she told me as we discussed her work, "findings that resting state networks are plastic and can be changed by pharmacological and behavioral interventions offer hope that effective treatments may help individuals mitigate symptoms and potentially improve cognitive function."

What this means is that deeply embedded expectations can be uprooted by changing your story and living the change. You are not stuck in the false truth of the past. The scientific term for the brain changing based on what you do and feel is "experience-dependent neuroplasticity." If you walk a new walk and feel new feelings, your brain will literally remold and rewire itself to erase the old way and create the new one. The process is both physical and psychological.

CHANGE YOUR THOUGHTS → CHANGE YOUR BEHAVIOR → RESHAPE YOUR BRAIN.

Change your thoughts. Humans have a "negative bias," which is an evolutionary tick, a holdover from caveman days when we were prey and had to assume that the rustling in the bushes really was a tiger and not a gentle, balmy breeze. Not only are we primed to scan the savanna (or the landscape of our lives) for trouble, when we spot trouble it's all we see. We fixate on the bad. Say your spouse or boss tells you 10 good things and 1 critical thing. It's human nature to forget about the praise and obsess about the criticism.

You have already been developing countermeasures against a negative bias by swapping negative assumptions for positive ones and good intentions. The false truth that said you didn't deserve happiness, were unworthy of it, or were inadequate? You are not attached to that anymore. You are instead focusing on what you're good at and what you have to offer. You combat slights by depersonalizing situations—third-person POV and 3-D empathy—and by keeping a mentality of reality. What is really happening in this moment? Is it good, bad, ugly, pretty, none of the above, all of the above? Scan your landscape for *everything*. Act as if you were a human radar, and zero in on the good in people, places, and situations.

Change your behavior. Every time you disconfirm your old story and reconfirm the new one, you are experiencing behavioral change in action. Level up by patting yourself on the back every time something goes well. Revel in success and happiness. Be your own cheerleader, even if it seems awkward and embarrassing. Remember, that awkward feeling means that you are breaking out of the trenches of the old story. It feels weird because it's different.

When you are able to come back after a fall, get a second date, land a job, not let your mother get under your skin, turn a marital spat into deeper appreciation for each other, celebrate it! Say, "Way to go, me! I'm awesome. I bounced back! I worked hard and got what I wanted!" You don't have to crow obnoxiously about your success in front of others, just sing your praises inside your head for at least 20 seconds to trigger a release of the "reward" hormone, dopamine. You'll start associating doing well with feeling good.

Change your brain. Feedback loops get deeper and more powerful with each instance. One "do well, feel good" experience helps build the next. The brain connections between synapses created by linking "do well" and "feel good" get brighter and deeper, while the old "I messed up, as usual" ones flicker out and disappear. The stronger the connections between synapses, the more quickly our neurons travel down those pathways, so you won't need huge glory to feel excellent about yourself. It takes some time, and a lot of repetition, but it is absolutely possible, at any age, to change your bias and shape your brain away from negativity and expected failure and instead toward reality and celebrated success. Neuroplasticity is real.

The brain reinforces the neural circuitry that we use time and time again. This happens automatically, but you can help the process along by giving your brain the opportunity to do its job. "Synaptic pruning" is what scientists call the process of clearing away old synapses to make room for new, better ones to grow, and they make a lot of gardening metaphors. I like a demolition model. When you stop using certain synapses, they dilapidate, like an old, neglected house. Certain proteins bind to the deteriorated synapses, marking them for destruction. Then glial and microglial cells, the wrecking balls of the brain, move in to do their job. Researchers aren't exactly sure how the process works, but they do know when it takes place: *during sleep.*

Your brain goes through a complete renovation while you're unconscious, bulldozing old connections and constructing shiny new ones. Unless you get adequate sleep, you can't build a new "house" or narrative, because the skeleton of the old one is blocking the way. Seven to eight hours a night will allow your brain to keep up with the pace of your insightful transformation.

Insight Through Meditation

One of the fastest ways to enhance every aspect of the Insight Cure is also the simplest. Go to a quiet place for few minutes, sit still, and take deep breaths. A meditation practice makes it easier to access memory, have a positive outlook, speed up the formation of new brain connections, and add folds in the brain regions that control emotions. Meditation is drug free, requires very little time, and can be done by anyone, nearly anywhere. The benefits have been proven by science.

Meditation reshapes the brain for emotional awareness and control. At UCLA, scientists used MRI machines to map brain geometry, aka gyrification (the wrinkles and folding of gray matter), of fifty long-term meditators, ages 24 to 71. The subjects' brains had more folding in the cortex's insula region that controls emotional awareness, decision making, and sense of self. A longer history of meditation correlated with more gyrification.[16] The practice of meditation changes the shape of the brain over time, giving you more control of your emotions and response to stress.

Meditation reshapes the brain for calm and compassion. Scientists from Harvard and Massachusetts General Hospital used MRI machines to measure the brains of 16 non-meditating subjects before and after an eight-week mindful stress-reduction program. *In just two months,* researchers noted significant increases in gray matter concentration in the hippocampus, cortex, and cerebellum, the regions that control learning, memory, emotional control, empathy, and stress regulation.[17]

Meditation floods the brain with happy hormones. There are four hormones of happiness: Dopamine (the "reward" hormone) is released when you accomplish something, receive positive feedback, or try new, exciting things. Serotonin (the "calm" hormone) makes you feel centered and relaxed. Oxytocin (the "love" hormone) is released when you feel content, safe, and close with loved ones. Endorphins (the "runner's high" hormones) reduce pain and increase well-being. All four alleviate stress, anxiety, and depression. All four are activated by meditation.

Why does meditation change the brain and flood it with happy chemicals? When you sit in silence while counting breaths and concentrating on stillness, you are free of past pain and future worries. In this relaxed yet focused state, you can rest and replenish and clear your mind of stuck emotions and stress. The more you do it, the easier it is to return to the calm and stillness, even when the world swirling around you.

BRAIN RESHAPING TOOL:

Meditation

The meditation technique I use and recommend is called *square breathing.*

1. Find a quiet place to sit comfortably on a chair or on the floor, with cushions or a blanket if necessary.

2. Close your eyes and begin concentrating on the rhythm of your inhalations and exhalations.

3. Picture a square in your mind's eye. As you inhale for a count of three or four, imagine air filling the

square. Hold the breath for three or four counts. As you exhale, imagine the air rushing out of the square for three or four counts. Repeat.

4. If your mind wanders, gently bring your thoughts back to the square.

5. Try to keep this up for two to five minutes. Strive for two five-minute meditations per day.

Insight: Mission Ongoing

A very common question I get from patients is "How will I know I'm cured?"

For alcoholics and drug addicts, there is no cure, only vigilant management of the chronic disease and constant reinforcement of effective recovery strategies.

People who use the Insight Cure *can* "cure" themselves of the dis-ease of their pathogenic belief and change their assumptions about life. But the cure can only be achieved with vigilance, maintenance, resilience, and further development of the new narrative. It's not enough to use insight to light your path once, twice, or a hundred times. The big fix occurs when you use the tools in this book so often that they become automatic. This is the *termination* stage of change. You become a success when you don't think about being one. You have control when you aren't trying to get it.

It might seem Zen. Mastery is a strange concept until you've experienced it, and then it's a bit mundane. You have been experiencing a new life for so long that it's just your life. You're "cured" when confidence and happiness aren't the "new normal" but just the way things are.

The Four Stages of Learning

As you continue your mission of mastery, the four stages of learning or competence will help you assess your growth.

1. **Unconscious incompetence.** You don't know why you can't do something, such as controlling your thoughts and behavior. You might not even know that there's a different, better way to live. If someone told you that happiness and success were possible, you wouldn't believe it and would reject any efforts to realize a new life.

2. **Conscious incompetence.** You know that you fail for a reason, even if you don't know how to correct it. You want control, and you understand that you've got a lot to learn before you gain mastery.

3. **Conscious competence.** You learn new skills and acquire the tools for success and happiness, but you're not great at using them. You have to focus, concentrate, practice, practice, practice, and be vigilant and mindful about improving.

4. **Unconscious competence.** You've learned a skill so well, you do it easily and automatically. You don't have to think about doing it, concentrating hard and practicing constantly. The skill is second nature.

By the time you get to unconscious competence, you'll be so busy living your life that you might not have the time or inclination to reflect on how far you've come. But at some point, after dealing with a crisis with aplomb or observing a self-sabotaging behavior in someone else, you might experience another insightful sinking feeling, another pull of gravity that roots you even more deeply into the person you've become.

You see the world—your extraordinary world—as a hopeful, acceptable place, full of potential, where you can breathe and be fully present.

You feel safe.

Your universe of social connections is ever expanding.

You have trained yourself to look for the good in everyone, especially yourself.

You allow people to reveal themselves to you as who they really are.

You allow trust to build over time.

No one in your life is holding you back. And if someone is, you know it and are choosing to tolerate them temporarily and for a healthy reason of which you are aware.

You feel in control much of the time.

You have trust in yourself that you can now respond intuitively to the situation at hand.

Your close friends are good for you, and you're good for them.

You have made peace with your feelings about your family.

You have forgiven yourself the negative associations you had from childhood.

You have a hopeful yet realistic outlook, looking for the best and dealing with the worst.

You are resilient. You bounce back.

You give back.

You openly share love.

The blocks to living out of your true inner self have been released.

SIX MONTHS AFTER

My deepest gratification as a therapist is when, six months after gaining insight, a patient says, "You know, things have been better for a while now. I don't know when it happened, but my whole life has changed." Here's where each of my patients was after six months of working on their Insight Cure.

Larry

Larry learned that he really did care about himself and his performance in life. He also learned that he needed to define a place for himself, a role to fulfill, and that there was a clear opportunity right in front of him. He's not working in support of his wife. "We are a team," he told me. "I don't have to be resentful." By testing his strengths of gratitude and appreciation, he convinced himself that she couldn't achieve the full measure of her success without him. "She's front office, I'm back office" is the way he liked to look at it. Larry scheduled speaking tours for his wife and negotiated plans and logistics. He came to think positively about being the man behind the scenes. And what about the affairs? "Nonexistent," he said. When the false truth was gone and he had insight into what drove him to have affairs, he lost the compulsion to have them.

Daria

Daria is still working in LA, but she is experiencing more steadiness in her life and more self-reliance. These go hand in hand. Her work has improved—better gigs with bigger productions. She realized that neediness stemmed from insecurity, and she has come to be able to depend on herself in the context of a few decent friendships in the movie industry and in her friend group of "my assembled family, the ones I choose." She has been able to let these few chosen ones prove themselves to be decent and present and trustworthy gradually and over some time. Presently, she has no relationship with her twin at all. As for her parents, Daria relates with them only superficially now. "It used to kill me, but it's just the way they like it," she said. "I never wanted to give up on my family, but they just aren't capable of behaving any differently."

Bobby

Bobby deepened his effective working relationships with people who could help him rebuild his business, but it wasn't easy. He lost his store and the community there that he felt he needed, both for himself ("I'm so damn lonely now") and for others. Despite his near financial ruin, Bobby continued to buy and sell vinyl records online and eventually persuaded a few music aficionados to become investors in setting up a new brick-and-mortar space. Bobby remained optimistic while he developed a basis for a more a realistic and sound future. "My new MO," he said, "is to no longer ask what I can do for others; it is to ask what others can do for me." He discovered that "it all works better when we all work together."

Leo

Once Leo unlocked his false truth, insight rushed in to fill the gaps in his life. He now has a better relationship with his parents. Using empathy, he sees that their survival instinct has been to keep their feelings bottled up. He doesn't feel anger toward them anymore for their reticence. He understands it. It's not how he chooses to live his life, but in his heart he respects his parents' choices and leaves it at that. He looks inside himself for the praise he needs, and through a new circle of friends and a new relationship, he's learning healthier ways to express his emotions. When in doubt, he takes the "humble" road and says to himself, "I'm no better than anyone. And no one is better than me. We're all doing the best we can with what we're given and what we understand."

Carrie

It's been several months since Carrie's car accident and her major insight breakthrough that asking for help isn't a sight of weakness but a way to strengthen herself and her relationships. She has worked hard to switch "overwhelmed" into "excited." A "difficult situation" is now an "interesting challenge." By actively testing her new narrative, Carrie has learned that being scared is just a part of life, like being happy, angry, and sad. She did shut down when her new boyfriend made emotional demands. "I knew exactly what was happening, and I could explain to him the reason for it," she said. She's also landed her first real job, at a tech company designing logos. "I still feel crushed if I'm criticized. But, again, I know what's going on, and I can step outside myself and see it clearly and recover more quickly. No more crying in the bathroom."

Claudia

Fortunately, Claudia came to differentiate her mother's "so inspiring" example from her own high standards. "I really don't feel I have to do my absolute best all the time. I can't actually, and it just generates too much disappointment," she said. Moreover, she has gotten much better at learning to ask people to do what they are capable of doing and no more. "Well, maybe a little bit more," she said with a twinkle in her eye. She went off by herself on several retreats in order to make headway on her art and her music. Coincidentally, a special relationship sparked with a woman she met on one of those retreats, a woman who "brings as much game as I do," Claudia shared with me. They have managed to work through some major logistical hurdles to align their lives and are now together. "I'm still too busy a lot of the time. I feel I have so much to do. Time is so precious. But it's so nice to feel that I'm not alone anymore and that I'm not going to be let down."

Steve

Steve ran into legal problems and got overwhelmed. His sliding-over-the-surface approach to life caught up with him when he was accused of a crime and failed to take the matter as seriously as needed. He was heavily penalized for being late to court and spent several nights in jail for contempt. But his steadfast nature helped him survive and, with the proper legal support, he got past this dire and distressing period. We did some more work on "squaring up with reality from the start," as he put it. He admitted he finally trusted me by saying, "I don't know what it takes, Doc, but I'm glad you do." The truth was, he did know what do to. He just didn't want to admit it.

Skylar

Skylar stopped her activities as an escort when she moved to Chicago and redirected herself to earn an MFA in writing from a top program. She has chosen to write about her journey and about the critical role of insight in her recovery. By applying the insight she gained and using her strengths and skills, Skylar wrote a memoir about her experiences that attracted the attention of a high-powered book agent. Several publishing houses are bidding for the rights to her story. She's made a success out of her deeply troubled past. In a very real sense, Skylar's new life is only just beginning.

The Sharp Focus on the Future

And what about you? Where will you be six months or a year after completing the eight-step enlightening, practical Insight Cure progression? I hope and trust that you'll be actively engaged with the continuing process of working through insight, being mindful of the fact that you've examined, disassembled, and replaced a horrible false truth with a wonderful, bright, refreshing, astonishing appreciation of your real, authentic self. You have in fact changed your story and changed your life. You couldn't possibly pat yourself on the back enough for undertaking such a monumental journey, one that I'm so glad to have taken with you.

This "cure" is very much like a medical procedure of localization, extraction, and reconstruction, such as the cure for a malformation in your hip. It's not enough to have the surgery. You also have to keep up with rehab and exercise. You have to mobilize in order to actively enjoy your splendidly reconstituted gait, thereby ensuring that you remain fully healthy, supple, and strong. You're not all the way better until you've lived with your powerful, unrestricted new outlook for a while, always checking in with it to make sure it's working just as it should. Occasionally, you will want to give it some supplemental power with a conscious boost of extra energy. Eventually, this process becomes the new normal, hardwired into your brain and fully automatic.

The way you nurture yourself along the way to unconscious competence, aka mastery, is to just be yourself—meaning your true self. Remind yourself daily of your strengths and virtues. Do this in a few breaths. Bring a healthy sense of your own capabilities and confidence with you into every challenge, relationship, and crisis. Trust yourself to make accurate assessments of who and what you are dealing with in the world.

You can judge the actions and intentions of others in a fair and compassionate way because by taking this journey, you have developed a balanced gaze. Whether you are reflecting on your inward experience or outward interactions, you have the ability now to proceed with greater aptitude and a positive attitude. Over time your second nature, which is really your true nature revealed, comes to feel completely natural. Your ability to be happier and more fulfilled is what will serve you as you discover what your purposeful and full life holds in store for you.

And the best part? You are excited about the future, have learned to trust your new intuitive ability when responding in real time to situations, and can be wonderfully at peace with having absolutely no idea just what comes next.

THE SCIENCE
BEHIND THE
INSIGHT CURE

I forged this eight-step integrated Insight Cure by taking the best concepts and tools from several different schools of applied psychology—addiction recovery therapy, attachment theory, Cognitive Behavior Therapy, control mastery theory, narrative therapy, positive psychology, Erikson's psychosocial development theory, and the transtheoretical model—and combining them in a unique way that, in my clinical experience, brings about lasting, meaningful change as effectively as possible. Throughout the book, I've discussed the principles of each and have directed you to explore more in-depth information about them in this section. Consider it a cheat sheet for the science you have used and will continue to use as you live out with insight.

Addiction Recovery Therapy

Addiction recovery therapy's main tenet is that you can't rely on willpower alone. Willpower is finite. Over the course of a day, you get tired of holding off. The willpower well runs dry. Another tenet of traditional recovery therapy is to change your life to avoid triggers, surround yourself with healthy people, and find a way to contribute to the good of society. Don't wait for trouble to find you. Run from it. If you're alone with your demons, go to a meeting. Don't let yourself get HALT (too hungry, angry, lonely, or tired) or your guard will come down. Insight is an important tool as well. Any good recovery therapy process will ask the deep questions: Why does the addict need to use drugs and alcohol in the first place? What is driving the addiction? Understanding what makes them vulnerable, however, doesn't always stop people from turning to substances again and again. There is also a habitual, learned response at play. We tend to do the same things over and over. Moving on to a new healthy routine without the old toxic element is hard, but it gets easier. As the saying goes, it's harder to get stopped than to stay stopped.

KEYWORDS

Willpower: Inner strength that dwindles over the course of the day.

HALT: Acronym for hungry, anger, lonely, and tired, which can all cause you to put yourself in dangerous situations that make you vulnerable to falling off the wagon.

Attachment Theory

In the 1960s, Dr. John Bowlby and Mary Ainsworth, Ph.D., developed the theory that a child's attachment to his parents determines the cause of his current and future psychological issues. They designated three main attachment styles—secure, anxious, and avoidant—and a few subcategories as well. If a child is securely attached to his parent, and the parent leaves him alone in a room (the "strange situation" experiment), the child will get upset but will be able to distract himself until the parent returns. When she does, he'll go right to her and allow her to soothe him. According to researchers, the child's behavior is a sign of consistent, loving parenting. On the other hand, a child with an avoidant attachment doesn't seem to care if his mother leaves the room, doesn't bother distracting himself, and ignores her when she returns, a major "tell" that the parenting has been inconsistent and unreliable, and an anxiously attached child does not know how to respond to the mother's return. Later on, researchers used childhood attachment styles as a way to predict and analyze adult romantic lives and to shed light on why people's relationships seem to follow similar patterns. A securely attached child is likely to grow up to have trusting, mutually satisfying partnerships. An anxiously attached child is likely to grow up to be distrustful, smothering, and in need of constant reassurance, driving partners away. An avoidantly attached child is likely to grow up to be dismissive of the importance of emotional intimacy, holding partners at arm's length and suppressing emotions in crisis.

KEYWORDS

Childhood attachment style: How you related as a child with a parent or caregiver.

Adult attachment style: How you relate as an adult to romantic partners.

Secure attachment: Trusting, open, and dependable.

Anxious attachment: Distrustful, insecure, clingy, and erratic.

Avoidant attachment: Dismissive, untrustworthy, and noncommittal.

Cognitive Behavior Therapy

Invented by Aaron Beck in the 1960s, Cognitive Behavior Therapy (CBT) is a results-oriented method of connecting the power of thought with emotions and actions. If you can learn to silence negative self-talk, and consciously edit negative assumptions through prescribed changes in the mechanics of what you do, you can actually change how you feel. It's all about becoming conscious of your thoughts and feelings by keeping records about them on a log sheet or in a notebook. With this collection of data, you can predict when negative thoughts and feeling will occur, gain awareness about what circumstances trigger them, and then, with behavioral training, overcome them. CBT is a short-term therapy, usually lasting only six or eight months, with a focus on practical application to change specific thought or behavioral patterns. Variations of CBT can apply to things like obsessive-compulsive behaviors (hand washing, hair pulling, skin excoriation), panic attacks, insomnia, and eating disorders.

KEYWORDS

Trigger: A situation or experience that activates negative thoughts, emotions, and behaviors, largely unconsciously.

Habituation: The process by which a way of acting or reacting becomes entrenched and largely unconscious.

Control Mastery Theory

Developed by Dr. Joseph Weiss and Harold Sampson, Ph.D., in the 1950s and '60s, control mastery theory (CMT) puts forth the concept of a *pathogenic belief,* or what I call a false truth. When you were a child (age seven or younger), bad or upsetting events created a misconception about who you are and how the world works. Based on these pathogenic beliefs, you developed an unconscious narrative, what I call the "old story," essentially a playbook about how you should behave to feel safe in light of the false truth. Throughout your life, you've been unconsciously "testing" the validity of your false truth. For example, a neglected child would unknowingly test and confirm the false truth "No one cares about me" by choosing distant, unreliable partners. She would unknowingly test and disprove it by finding and staying in healthy, trusting relationships. Testing is a major component of CMT. The patient tests the therapist in session by re-creating the childhood trauma, assuming the role of the child and putting the doctor in the role of parent, or vice versa.

KEYWORDS

Pathogenic belief: A misconception formed in childhood that shaped your behavior; also called a *maladaptive belief.*

Unconscious narrative: The story you didn't realize you had been telling yourself since childhood about who you are and your place in the world.

Testing: Unconsciously seeking to confirm or disconfirm your false truth, in the real world or in therapy.

Narrative Therapy

Narrative therapy (NT) was developed in the 1970s and '80s, mainly by Michael White, an Australian social worker, and New Zealand social worker David Epston. It's all about creating a strong identity by taking a close look at your past to determine what you're good at and applying those skills and talents in life. By compiling a list of only effective qualities, you are *coauthoring* a narrative or story about who you are and how you can live a successful, happy life, with yourself as the main character. By looking at the past (White called this *re-membering*), you can find *unique outcomes*, or times in your life when have already embodied your coauthored character. By seeing yourself as a character and your life as a story, you can depersonalize or *externalize* a problem as something outside of yourself, as a plot twist that is making things hard for you but has nothing to do with your actual character, which is defined by good qualities and solid values. As White said, "The person is not the problem. The problem is the problem."

KEYWORDS

Coauthorship: Creating a character and story for yourself, by yourself, based on your virtues and strengths.

Re-membering: Looking back at your life with insight.

New narrative: The story of your life going forward as a strong and virtuous hero; also called a *new story*.

Unique outcomes: Times in the past when you closely matched your coauthored character.

Exceptional experiences: Times when you weren't locked and blocked by the unconscious narrative, though usually only temporarily.

Externalization: Stepping outside yourself to see the problem as an impartial observer, separating it from the assumptions you have about your identity.

Positive Psychology

In the late 1990s, my Harvard colleague Martin Seligman started positive psychology. His premise was that instead of psychologists treating only the misery and suffering of severely dysfunctional and disordered patients, why not figure out ways to increase happiness and fulfillment for regular people? According to his research, you can build a foundation for happiness by developing personal strengths and a positive, future-oriented outlook on life, being mindful about your emotions, and devoting your energies to things that give you a feeling of proficiency and pride. In collaboration with Christopher Peterson, Seligman came up with a list of 6 virtue categories and the 24 strengths that fall into them. If you live by your strengths, you'll feel good about yourself, and those good vibes reinforce themselves. If you have PERMA—positive emotions, engagement in life, positive relationships, meaning, and accomplishment—you are well positioned to flourish.

KEYWORDS

PERMA: Acronym for positive emotions, engagement in life, positive relationships, meaning, and accomplishment, all the things you need to flourish.

Virtues: The six categories of human goodness—wisdom, courage, humanity, transcendence, justice, and moderation.

Strengths: Twenty-four traits that fall into the six virtue categories (see pages 157–158).

Psychosocial Development Theory

German-born American social psychologist Erik Erikson developed this theory in the 1950s and '60s. It pertains to the concept of *ego identity*, your sense of self (ego), of having a unique identity, which is based on your interactions with other people. Your psyche has a one-of-a-kind fingerprint. Erikson specified eight developmental stages based on age ranges. During each stage, you will interact with others (parents, teachers, peers, etc.), learning lessons that will ideally lead to gaining skills, aka *virtues*, to prepare you for further development in the next stage. However, if you don't learn what you need to, your development will be impaired or thwarted. You can't go back in time and change your ego identity so that you are better adjusted, but you can study the theory of psychosocial development to get some ideas of where your life took a bad turn and then relearn the lessons associated with that stage in order to improve your outlook.

KEYWORDS

Ego: Your sense of self.

Identity: Your unique psychosocial developmental fingerprint.

Virtues: The favorable outcomes learned at each stage of development.

Transtheoretical Model

Professor of psychology at the University of Rhode Island James O. Prochaska, along with his colleague Carlo DiClemente, developed the transtheoretical model, otherwise known as the stages of change, in the 1970s. According to Prochaska, change is a process that has six distinct stages, and in order to successfully adopt any new, healthier behavior, an individual will need strategies for each of the six stages. The six stages are precontemplation, contemplation, preparation, action, maintenance, and termination.

KEYWORDS

Precontemplation: The period before an individual thinks about changing.

Contemplation: When an individual is thinking about changing.

Preparation: A person is ready to change and begins taking preliminary steps to do so.

Action: A person changes old behaviors and adopts new behaviors.

Maintenance: A person sticks with the new behaviors for at least six months.

Termination: The individual has changed completely.

Relapse: A setback that can occur during the action and maintenance stages.

ENDNOTES

Step One

1. See R. Aunger and V. Curtis, "The Anatomy of Motivation: An Evolutionary-Ecological Approach," *Biological Theory* 8, no. 1 (July 2013): 49–63.

2. Jim Taylor, "Motivation: The Drive to Change," *Huffpost* blog, Mach 11, 2012, http://www.huffingtonpost.com/dr-jim-taylor/motivation_b_1179582.html.

Step Two

3. J. N. Rouder et al., "An Assessment of Fixed-Capacity Models of Visual Working Memory," *Proceedings of the National Academy of Sciences of the United States of America* 105, no. 16 (April 2008): 5975–79.

4. Vincent J. Felitti et al., "Relationship of Childhood Abuse and Household Dysfunction to Many of the Leading Causes of Death in Adults: The Adverse Childhood Experiences (ACE) Study," *American Journal of Preventative Medicine* 14, no. 4 (May 1998): 245–58.

5. Robert Anda, quoted in David Bornstein, "Putting the Power of Self-Knowledge to Work," Fixes column, *New York Times*, August 23, 2016, www.nytimes.com/2016/08/23/opinion/putting-the-power-of-self-knowledge-to-work.html.

6. Sue Gerhardt, *Why Love Matters: How Affection Shapes a Baby's Brain*, (New York: Routledge, 2014).

Step Three

7. Cindy Hazan and Phillip Shaver, "Romantic Love Conceptualized as an Attachment Process," *Journal of Personality and Social Psychology* 52, no. 3 (March 1987): 511–24.

8. Patricia A. Frazier et al., "Adult Attachment Style and Partner Choice: Correlational and Experimental Findings," *Personal Relationships* 3, no. 2 (June 1996): 117–36.

9. Lee A. Kirkpatrick and Cindy Hazan, "Attachment Styles and Close Relationships: A Four-Year Prospective Study," *Personal Relationships* 1, no. 2 (June 1994): 123–42.

Step Four

10. Carl G. Jung, "The Association Method," trans. A. A. Brill, *American Journal of Psychology* 21 (1910): 219–69.

11. M. H. Klein et al., *The Experiencing Scale: A Research and Training Manual* vol. 1, 56–63 (Madison: Wisconsin Psychiatric Institute, 1969).

12. Els van der Helm et al., "REM Sleep De-potentiates Amygdala Activity to Previous Emotional Experiences," *Current Biology* 21, no. 23 (December 6, 2011), 2029–32.

Step Five

13. Joseph Campbell, *The Hero with a Thousand Faces*, 3rd ed. (Novato, CA: New World Library, 2008), 18.

Step Seven

14. Examples come from Steven A. Foreman's excellent essay "The Significance of Turning Passive into Active in Control Mastery Theory," *Journal of Psychotherapy Practice and Research* 5, no. 2 (spring 1996): 106–21.

Step Eight

15. Susan Whitfield-Gabrieli and Judith M. Ford, "Default Mode Network Activity and Connectivity in Psychopathology," *Annual Review of Clinical Psychology* 8 (2012): 49–76.

16. Eileen Luders et al., "The Unique Brain Anatomy of Meditation Practitioners: Alterations in Cortical Gyrification," *Frontiers in Human Neuroscience*, published online February 29, 2012, http://journal.frontiersin.org/article/10.3389/fnhum.2012.00034.

17. Britta K. Hölzel et al., "Mindfulness Practice Leads to Increases in Regional Brain Gray Matter Density," *Psychiatry Research* 19, no. 1 (January 2011), 36–43.

INDEX

ACKNOWLEDGMENTS

There's an unlikely chain of humans that accounts for this book coming to be.

A few years ago, Sanjiv Chopra gently encouraged me to keep on with my writing. Jeanine Pirro invited me to help with hers, and in so doing introduced me to the great Valerie Frankel, my new BFF, whose talents are on every page of *The Insight Cure.*

Through Valerie, I met the spirited and determined Alex Glass, and soon thereafter we were off to the races with the endorsement and support of Patty Gift and her spectacular team at Hay House. I am grateful to Lisa Cheng and Rachel Shields for their superb detail work on the manuscript, Grace Tobin for her illustrations, and to Richelle Fredson for her wise counsel and PR talents.

I'd like to humbly acknowledge key role models who paved the way for me: Ezra Sharp, Bill Bourne, Buddy Bates, Robert Coles, E. O. Wilson, James Hammill, Steve Purcell, Victor Reus, and Sanjiv Chopra. Thank you all, gentlemen.

I'd also like to acknowledge all my devoted patients from whom I have learned so much about how to do my job with sensitivity, specificity, and devotion. Thank you for trusting me with your lives.

Great gratitude to my daughters Ashley and Else; my wonderful wife, Elline; and of course my mom—the four navigation points on my life's compass.

And thanks to the one non-human in the chain, my Bedlington buddy, Jesse.

ABOUT THE AUTHOR

John Sharp, M.D., is a seasoned medical professional, board certified psychiatrist, and media expert. He is on the faculty at the Harvard Medical School and David Geffen School of Medicine at UCLA and has treated patients clinically for 20 years. He is the author of *The Emotional Calendar* and a blogger for *Psychology Today* and the Huffington Post. He is also an elected member of the American College of Psychiatrists and served as a standing member of the Examining Committee of the American Board of Psychiatry Association and the Academy of Psychosomatic Medicine. Dr. Sharp divides his time between Boston and Los Angeles, and you can visit him online at johnsharpmd.com.

Hay House Titles of Related Interest

YOU CAN HEAL YOUR LIFE, the movie,
starring Louise Hay & Friends
(available as a 1-DVD program, an expanded 2-DVD set,
and an online streaming video)
Learn more at www.hayhouse.com/louise-movie

THE SHIFT, the movie,
starring Dr. Wayne W. Dyer
(available as a 1-DVD program, an expanded 2-DVD set,
and an online streaming video)
Learn more at www.hayhouse.com/the-shift-movie

———

THE MAP:
Finding the Magic and Meaning
in the Story of Your Life,
by Colette Baron-Reid

THE POWER OF NAMING:
A Journey Toward Your Soul's Indigenous Nature,
by Melanie Dewberry

SH#T YOUR EGO SAYS:
Strategies to Overthrow Your Ego
and Become the Hero of Your Story,
by James McCrae

All of the above are available at your local bookstore,
or may be ordered by contacting Hay House (see next page).

———

We hope you enjoyed this Hay House book. If you'd like to receive our online catalog featuring additional information on Hay House books and products, or if you'd like to find out more about the Hay Foundation, please contact:

Hay House, Inc., P.O. Box 5100, Carlsbad, CA 92018-5100
(760) 431-7695 or (800) 654-5126
(760) 431-6948 (fax) or (800) 650-5115 (fax)
www.hayhouse.com® • www.hayfoundation.org

———

Published and distributed in Australia by:
Hay House Australia Pty. Ltd., 18/36 Ralph St., Alexandria NSW 2015
Phone: 612-9669-4299 • *Fax:* 612-9669-4144 • www.hayhouse.com.au

Published and distributed in the United Kingdom by:
Hay House UK, Ltd., Astley House, 33 Notting Hill Gate, London W11 3JQ
Phone: 44-20-3675-2450 • *Fax:* 44-20-3675-2451 • www.hayhouse.co.uk

Published in India by: Hay House Publishers India,
Muskaan Complex, Plot No. 3, B-2, Vasant Kunj, New Delhi 110 070
Phone: 91-11-4176-1620 • *Fax:* 91-11-4176-1630 • www.hayhouse.co.in

Distributed in Canada by:
Raincoast Books, 2440 Viking Way, Richmond, B.C. V6V 1N2
Phone: 1-800-663-5714 • *Fax:* 1-800-565-3770 • www.raincoast.com

———

Access New Knowledge.
Anytime. Anywhere.

Learn and evolve at your own pace
with the world's leading experts.

www.hayhouseU.com